THE NAUGHTY 90s

GW00691110

MIKE LEPINE
AND
MARK LEIGH

ARROW BOOKS

Arrow Books Limited

20 Vauxhall Bridge Road, London, SW1V 2SA

An imprint of the Random Century Group

London · Melbourne · Sydney · Auckland · Johannesburg
and agencies throughout the world

First Published 1990 © Mike Lepine and Mark Leigh 1990

Designed by Graham Davis Associates
Designers Graham Davis and Kevin Ryan
Illustrations Jim Robbins
All illustrations © Jim Robbins 1990

Photographs by Philippa Hatton
and Mark Leigh with Mike Lepine
*Photographs © Philippa Hatton,
Mark Leigh and Mike Lepine 1990*

Cover illustration by Mike Terry

From the authors of
*The Complete Revenge Kit, How To Be A Complete Bastard,
How To Be A Complete Bitch* and *The Book Of Revelations.*

Special thanks to

Asterix the Rottweiler
John Barford
Deborah Beale
Maggie Burke
Mrs Burke's apparition masks
  by Vic Door and Creepers
Rita Cash
Robert Cash
John Choopani
Neil Choopani
Stephen Choopani
Judy Copeland
Robert Ewen
Paul Ewen
Jeanne Ewen
Kevin Facer
Aemonn Flynn
Harry and Kathy Firman
Peggy and Andrew Fraser

Margy Frost
Frosts of Wimbledon
  (Seamus, Hardy and Carole)
Gladys
Harrie Green
Tony Harris
Graham Hart
Andrea Hatton
Mary Hatton
Philippa Hatton
Kathleen Holland
Honey the Rabbit
Sara, Mike and Sophie Howell
Steve Isbister
Lil Kelly
Bob Kelly
Alastair King
Ashley Kopitko
Gill and Neville Landau

Jonathan Landau
Michael Landau
Jonathan Law
Adam Leigh
Debbie Leigh
Miriam Leigh
Philip Leigh
Eileen and Harold Lepine
Jo Marchment
Steven Markham
Ann Martin
Mirrabeau's Wine Bar, Harrow
Diane Mumberson
Kirsty Murray
Aimee Oram
Raymond Oram
Tracey Oram
Paddington
Imogen Parker

Chris Phillips
Melanie Pomper
Rachel Power
Caroline Quy
Janine Roma
Darren Rose
Chris Saville
Tim Scott
Adam Sherman
Andrew Short
Mandy and Peter Speck
Alan Spiers
Daryl Sutch
Bert Turner
Valentino
Wealdstone Football Club
Tracy Wheeler
Neil Wilkinson

All the psychics and future events depicted in *The Naughty 90s*
are entirely fictitious. No resemblance to any person living or
dead has been intended nor should any be inferred.

This book is sold subject to the condition that it shall
not, by way of trade or otherwise, be lent, resold, hired out,
or otherwise circulated without the publisher's prior consent
in any form of binding or cover other than that in which it
is published and without a similar condition including
this condition being imposed on the subsequent purchaser

Typesetting by Roger Walker Graphic Design

Printed and bound in Great Britain by
The Guernsey Press Co Ltd, Guernsey, C.I.

ISBN 0 09 969630 4

INTRODUCTION

We are sitting in Madame Mystique's Sanctum Sanctorum in Gladstone Road, Dagenham, anxiously awaiting our first brush with the supernatural.

Madame Mystique calls for absolute silence as she consults her crystal ball. We feel something powerful start to build up. Raw energy, crackling... hot and fetid... All at once, a sulphurous wind of supernatural intensity rips through the room, throwing the curtains wide open. The candles splutter and go out...

...Embarrassed, we apologise for consuming a half-dozen Wimpy Spicy Beanburgers immediately prior to our consultation.

'See!' she cackles. 'Look at the images forming in the glass! You are writers!' We are not impressed. Anyone could tell that from our cheap clothes and the fact that we drove here in a 1972 Morris Marina.

'Ohhh... you are exceptionally talented authors, having written the four funniest comedy books ever seen on the face of this planet – *The Complete Revenge Kit, The Book of Revelations, How To Be a Complete Bitch* and *How To Be a Complete Bastard*... and you have your own section in the *Guinness Book of Records* under *Outstanding Achievements and Prodigious Feats in the Trouser Area!* I'm right, aren't I?'

She is one hundred per cent accurate. Now we are astounded.

'And you want me to predict what your next book is going to be... Am I right?' We nod, dumbfounded.

'Your next book shall contain psychic predictions for the 1990s. I see it all! It will be called *The Naughty 90s* and, to research it, you shall plunge head-first into a world of dread terror, where the nonsensical and insane shall seem commonplace!'

It doesn't scare us – we're used to dealing with the publishing industry...

The book you now hold in your hand contains dozens of those predictions. Astounding glimpses of the future torn from the misty veils of space and time – or just a load of old bollocks?

You, the reader, must decide for yourself...

WILL THE CHANNEL TUNNEL EVER BE COMPLETED?

'I'm not a psychic!' insists Laura Cooke. 'There's just something badly wrong with my telephone and I can't get British Telecom to fix it because, they say, they don't give a stuff!' Confused? So were we. After all, we weren't researching a book on British Telecom – we'd already written *How to Be a Complete Bastard*...

'The strange thing is, I get crossed lines... with the future. 'Every time I try to call someone, I hear telephone conversations between the British and French architects of the Channel Tunnel Project. I know it's the future because they're talking about how the opening ceremony went wrong!'

We look at her transcripts. They read like pure fantasy and we're about to write her off as just another charlatan... until she produces her phone bill. It's in the millions – exactly what you'd expect for calls connected eight years into the future, paying for every off-peak and standard minute along the way!

It's on the big day – the grand opening of the Channel Tunnel – when trouble starts. The chief British architect, Sir Raymond Hugo Parker, calls his French counterpart, Francois Duchampe...

LAURA COOKE

SIR RAYMOND: Hello, Francois!

FRANCOIS: Sir Raymond! *Comment ca va?*

SIR RAYMOND: Er, I'm fine, Francois… look, it's rather embarrassing. I've got the Duchess of York here, waiting to declare the Channel Tunnel officially open…

FRANCOIS: She is nice, eh, the Duchess? *Formidable! Je suis en amour avec sa derriere! C'est grande! C'est magnifique! Je voudrais…*

SIR RAYMOND: Look, the Duchess of York is a very busy woman. She's due to go skiing tonight and the snow's fast disappearing at Kloisters, so she'd like to get the opening ceremony over and done with as quickly as possible. The problem is, we haven't heard a word from your men on the other side yet. Where are they?

FRANCOIS: Er, Sir Raymond, I think you had better know that we haven't… er… well, we haven't actually started digging our side of the tunnel yet…

SIR RAYMOND: Francois, you were meant to have started six years ago!

FRANCOIS: We did. But… ah… we didn't like it very much, so we filled it in and have decided to start all over again… and get it right this time! The country which has astonished the world with the architectural splendour of *La Tour Eiffel* could never accept such a second-rate tunnel!

SIR RAYMOND: Oh my God!

FRANCOIS: It's going to be very nice! It's going to be perfectly round this time instead of sort of funny at the top. Your Duchess would not have wanted to open a nasty horrid asymmetrical tunnel, I am sure! She would have spat upon it in derision!

SIR RAYMOND: Francois… I am speechless… What am I going to tell the Duchess?

FRANCOIS: Tell her to come back some other time.

SIR RAYMOND: Oh God, this is so humiliating!

FRANCOIS: You would have felt much worse, Sir Raymond, had your Duchess broken through into our tunnel and cried out, 'This tunnel is an abcess on the bottom of the construction industry in general and the European construction industry in particular! I have soiled my dainty Royal hands in giving birth to this irregular, asymmetrical monstrosity of no worth whatsoever! I would rather have opened a tin of cat food! A dustbin! Something septic and putrescent! I would rather have burst a vast pustule than open this tunnel! I hate it! I hate it!'

SIR RAYMOND: I am going to go and lie down now, Francois.

FRANCOIS: *Bonsoir*, Sir Raymond. I will make you a nice tunnel. You will see.

(CLICK)

Sir Raymond does not give up there and then…

SIR RAYMOND: Hello, Francois, it's Sir Raymond. How are things going?

FRANCOIS: Oh, *tres bien, merci* Sir Raymond!

SIR RAYMOND: Excellent! Tell me, how far have you got now?

FRANCOIS: Oh, a long way!

SIR RAYMOND: How far is that, Francois?

FRANCOIS: Oh… sort of… hmmmm… a long way. It is all going very well!

SIR RAYMOND: A kilometre?

FRANCOIS: Hard to tell.

SIR RAYMOND: Half a kilometre?

FRANCOIS: Hard to tell.

SIR RAYMOND: A metre? A centimetre? A millimetre?

FRANCOIS: Hard to tell.

SIR RAYMOND: You have started it, haven't you?

FRANCOIS: Of course! Hold on, I shall shout out to my foreman: *Louis! Quelle longitude a t'elle?*

LOUIS: *Qu'est ce que c'est?*

FRANCOIS: *La tunnel; quelle longitude?*

LOUIS: *Quoi tunnel?*

FRANCOIS:	He says a long way, Sir Raymond. Very far!
SIR RAYMOND:	How far is that, Francois?
FRANCOIS:	He doesn't know. Louis is a superb foreman, but he has no sense of length. Height he doesn't do too badly on, but length, he cannot estimate at all…
SIR RAYMOND:	Francois, is there anybody who can tell me how long your end of the tunnel is?
FRANCOIS:	Well, Jean-Marc is good at estimating length. Height and breadth, he has his limitations… But length, I think so… To him, it comes easy. He is lucky.
SIR RAYMOND:	Can I talk to him, Francois?
FRANCOIS:	No. He has gone home with a cold.
	(There is an explosive noise from Sir Raymond; then the line goes dead)

SIR RAYMOND:	Hello, Francois?
FRANCOIS:	No, he is dead!
SIR RAYMOND:	Francois, I know that's you…
FRANCOIS:	Oh… Sir Raymond! Ha Ha! I thought you were wanting the other Francois… who is dead.
SIR RAYMOND:	How is the tunnel going, Francois?
FRANCOIS:	Oh, you know; *comme ci, comme ca*…
SIR RAYMOND:	Is work actually going on as we speak, Francois?
FRANCOIS:	Er… no, not as such, no. Gaston has broken his shovel and we are waiting for a new one to arrive from Lyon!
SIR RAYMOND:	You've stopped excavating because of that?
FRANCOIS:	Sir Raymond, please, I am doing everything in my power. I have lent my bicycle to Gaston who, even as we speak, is now pedalling steadfastly towards Lyon to purchase a new shovel… one which will never break again!

SIR RAYMOND: But Lyon's hundreds of miles away, Francois…

FRANCOIS: It is all right, Sir Raymond; he has a packed lunch and a very good road map!

SIR RAYMOND: That's not what I meant, Francois! Damn it man, why can't he just buy a shovel in the nearest town!

FRANCOIS: Do you know nothing of France, Sir Raymond? Why, the shovelsmiths of Lyon are renowned throughout the civilised world for the skills they bring to their ancient art! Do you want another inferior tunnel that we have to abandon?

SIR RAYMOND: Of course not, no…

FRANCOIS: The last tunnel was spoiled beyond redemption because we tried to cut corners by using cheap spades! Cheap spades from England, as I recall! Never again! We will use only the best and build the perfect tunnel, even if it takes us one hundred years! One thousand years! Time is of no importance!

SIR RAYMOND: Francois, I am going to talk to my prime minister about all this. I'm not exactly filled with confidence about your efforts to complete the tunnel.

FRANCOIS: Don't you dare to say that to Gaston after he has cycled all the way to Lyon and back to purchase his shovel! It is raining here! He only has a T-shirt on and is no doubt drenched to the bone but cycling relentlessly on, thinking only of the tunnel, which means so much to him!

SIR RAYMOND: Goodnight, Francois.

(CLICK)

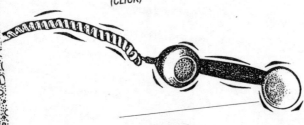

SIR RAYMOND: Hello, Francois?

FRANCOIS: Yes, Sir Raymond?

SIR RAYMOND: Francois, I think it's time we started being honest with each other, don't you? The prime minister wrote to your president and got her letter back, marked *'Not known at this address'*. Doesn't that strike you as odd, Francois? Just a little, maybe?

Do you know what I think, Francois? I think you French have no intention of building this tunnel!

FRANCOIS: Of course we do! We just don't rush things, unlike you English! We practise in our construction techniques what we practise in *l'amour*. Savour it! Make that moment last!

SIR RAYMOND: You're a lying little French shit, Francois!

FRANCOIS: Oh, so now it all comes out, eh! Your English racism! Stuff your tunnel up your monarchy, you English piece of staleness, you! You are right. We French never, ever intended to build our side of the tunnel – because we do not want ever, ever, ever to be joined to your England with its pints and quarts and soccer hooligans and polyester suits and MFI furniture and your F W Woolworth's and your chicken and chips and cockney rhyming slang which makes no sense at all and Benny Hill and spankings and your M25 and driving on the silly side of the road and your arrogance and your ugly bastard language which you think is so good, and your piddly little Post Office Tower and your flag which is impossible to draw correctly and your Sunday papers and your Derek Jameson, your ridiculous Royal Family and train spotting and cricket and 'Tits out for the lads' and dancing around your handbags and Guy Fawkes and Morris dancing and beer guts and darts and snooker on television all the time!

SIR RAYMOND: Er… You seem to have a very fair point there, Francois. I'll take it up with the prime minister. Goodnight, Francois.

FRANCOIS: *Bonsoir*, Sir Raymond.

(CLICK)

TRANSVESTITES UNITED!

'Are you the boys who've come to see my pubes?' says psychic Arthur Bunting, as he opens the door of his Peckham council flat. 'Come into the bathroom with me.'

We shudder. 'I bet you've never seen anything like this.' With our eyes tightly closed we agree. But then curiosity gets the better of us. What we see is not what we were expecting. Thank God. Mr Bunting is poking about in the plug hole with a pair of tweezers and a cotton bud.

'Look at this crinkly black one entwined with the one that looks a bit like New Zealand.' Mr Bunting points to the bath and continues enthusiastically. 'They're both stuck to that nail clipping by the blob of toe-jam, and there's an old scab resting precariously on the whole arrangement. That means something to do with football. Go on, take a close look.'

'Thank you, but we can see perfectly well from over here by the bathroom door,' we tell him.

Mr Bunting continues his painstaking investigation. 'Do you know what *that* means?' It isn't immediately obvious. But to Mr Bunting, the assorted debris in his plughole is telling him that football hooliganism will increase dramatically during the 1990s. The Government will decide that the only way to effectively stamp this out will be to discourage any red-blooded males from attending...

ARTHUR BUNTING

The compulsory renaming of all football league clubs will discourage supporters in droves. How many self-respecting fans are going to stand on the terraces on a bitterly cold and rainy day, waving their scarves and chanting, 'COME ON YOU SMEGGIES!'.

Division I

	HOME				AWAY			
	P	W	D	L	W	D	L	Pts
1 Liverpool Hermaphrodites	33	10	6	1	8	3	5	63
2 Everton Masturbators...........	32	9	6	2	8	5	2	62
3 Tottenham Infected Dongs...	33	11	3	3	5	4	7	55
4 Arsenal Smeggies	32	10	3	2	5	5	7	53
5 Norwich Little Willies...........	32	11	2	4	5	3	7	53
6 Wimbledon Impotents...........	33	9	5	2	4	8	5	52
7 Luton Geldings......................	32	10	5	2	4	4	7	51
8 Nottingham Eunuchs.............	32	9	5	2	4	6	6	50
9 Watford Premature Ejaculators........................	33	8	2	6	7	3	7	50
10 Coventry Plane Spotters	33	8	6	3	4	5	7	47
11 Manchester Haemorhoids.....	31	8	6	2	4	4	7	46
12 Southampton Tossers...........	33	8	5	4	3	8	5	46
13 Sheffield Tories....................	33	9	4	4	3	5	8	45
14 Chelsea Cocksuckers	32	8	6	1	3	5	9	44
15 West Ham Monotesticulars..................	33	8	4	4	2	7	8	41
16 Queens Park Cretins	33	8	3	5	3	4	10	40
17 Newcastle Nancies...............	33	8	5	4	2	4	10	39
18 Oxford Dickbreaths	32	6	7	2	4	1	12	38
19 Charlton Self-Abusers	33	7	5	4	1	8	8	37
20 Derby Cross Dressers...........	33	8	4	4	2	3	12	37
21 Portsmouth Bi's....................	33	5	7	4	3	5	9	36

New regulations will ensure that all teams have to turn out and play their matches with a completely new style of kit… women's clothing.

GROUP PLC

MILLWALL FOOTBALL CLUB

INCORPORATING THE FREDDIE MERCURY APPRECIATION SOCIETY

MEMBERSHIP NO: _4356/PO. OF_

NAME: _GARY HARDMAN_

OCCUPATION: _PLASTERER_

SIGNATURE: _Gary Hardman_

In the event of an accident (however minor and insignificant it might seem) and no matter how much I protest, like even if I try to remove this badge, please amputate my penis without anaesthetic and burn it.

ADMITTANCE WILL NOT BE PERMITTED UNLESS THIS MEMBERSHIP CARD IS PRESENTED AT THE TURNSTILE. SPECTATORS WILL BE EJECTED FROM THE GROUND UNLESS THE CARD IS DISPLAYED IN A VERY PROMINENT POSITION DURING THE ENTIRE GAME.

No one without an identity card will be admitted to football matches.

EDUCATION IN CRISIS!

The GCSE examination, introduced in 1988, was designed to hide the fact that kids were no longer anywhere near bright enough to get O levels.

Kids like sixteen-year-old Darren Dixon from Harrow Weald, who has never passed anything in his life, except for his cycling proficiency test and water.

Although blessed with a sixth sense (possibly because he seems to be lacking in the other five), Darren's psychic powers were not strong enough to let him foresee the right answers at school.

What he can foresee, however, is an urgent need to replace the GCSE exam with an even simpler one, which tomorrow's kids might have the slimmest chance of getting through and which won't inconvenience their social lives.

This is the sort of typical exam paper of the 1990s that Darren saw in his vision...

DARREN
DIXON

SECONDARY SCHOOL EXAMINATION BOARD

GENERAL CERTIFICATE – JUNE 1994

Name: *Gazzer Parrish*

School: *ST. Bartolomews*

Candidate No: *6969 WHORRR!!!*

Answer all questions. Time allowed: 3 hours.

Candidates are reminded of the need to get as many questions right as possible. If you are stuck on a question, please summon the invigilator by raising your hand. He or she will then come to your desk and give you a bloody big clue.

HISTORY
When did you last go on holiday? *Last summer*

GEOGRAPHY
Where to? *Malaga, wiv me mates*

ART
Who is this?

Some old tart

ECONOMICS
How much is a Big Mac and regular fries? *£1.27*

MATHS
If you and your girlfriend stay in the house alone, how many people are there? *4*

MUSIC
Name one member of Bros. *Luke. what a wanker!*

COMPUTER SCIENCE
Can you get Air Strike *for an Atari 4000 system?* *Yes*

PHYSICS
What sort of batteries does a Sony Walkman DD58 take? *One HP14*

BIOLOGY
Give the medical names for these parts.

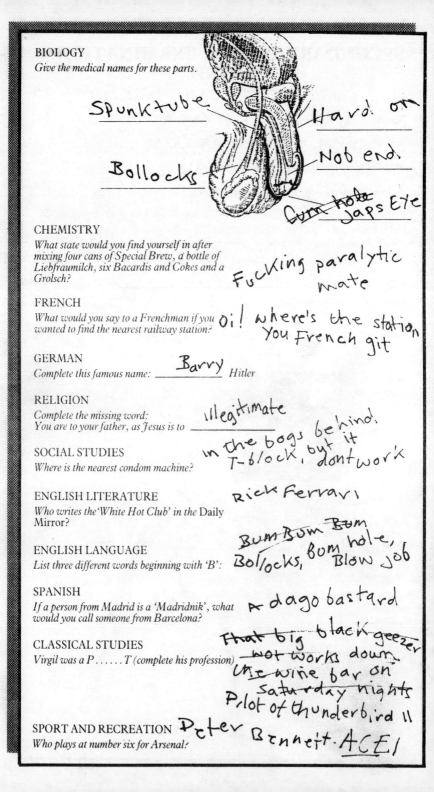

Spunktube

Hard. on

Bollocks

Nob end.

~~Cum hole~~ Japs Eye

CHEMISTRY
What state would you find yourself in after mixing four cans of Special Brew, a bottle of Liebfraumilch, six Bacardis and Cokes and a Grolsch?

Fucking paralytic mate

FRENCH
What would you say to a Frenchman if you wanted to find the nearest railway station?

Oi! where's the station you French git

GERMAN
Complete this famous name: ____Barry____ *Hitler*

RELIGION
Complete the missing word:
You are to your father, as Jesus is to ____illegitimate____

SOCIAL STUDIES
Where is the nearest condom machine?

in the bogs behind T-block, but it dont work

ENGLISH LITERATURE
Who writes the 'White Hot Club' in the Daily Mirror?

Rick Ferrari

ENGLISH LANGUAGE
List three different words beginning with 'B':

~~Bum Bum Bum~~
Bollocks, Bum hole, Blow job

SPANISH
If a person from Madrid is a 'Madridnik', what would you call someone from Barcelona?

A dago bastard

CLASSICAL STUDIES
Virgil was a P......T (complete his profession)

~~That big black geezer wot works down~~ the wine bar on Saturday nights Pilot of thunderbird II

SPORT AND RECREATION
Who plays at number six for Arsenal?

Peter Bennett. ACE!

With education authorities giving up all hope of getting standards to improve, kids will begin the long slide into a life of no hope and delinquency – destined to be nothing but Woolworth's employees.

By 1995 Darren sees the personal school timetable of a typical fourteen-year-old looking like this...

	MON	TUES	WED	THURS	FRI
PERIOD 1	Maths	Eng	FMF	BO	SL
PERIOD 2	BO	Eng	Geog	Comp.Sci	FMF
BREAK	Comp.Sci	SBB	BSJ	RDM	FST
PERIOD 3	Art	Maths	FMF	PWM	HSM
PERIOD 4	Art	HSM	Eng	Hist	SCJ
LUNCH	FST	HSM	BSJ	FMF	SCJ
PERIOD 5	SBB	SOQ	SOQ	BO	Chem
PERIOD 6	Hist	MSS	French	Gen.Studies	Chem
PERIOD 7	FMP	PTI	French	BSJ	FMF

KEY:

```
BO  = Bunk off
BSJ = Bundle  with St James school
FMF = Give Mary Field of 4B one in the girl's bogs
FST = Fight with 'Swotty' Townsend
HSM = Hang out in the shopping mall and nick stuff
MSS = Make suggestive signs outside Miss 'Whopper'
      Harris's class
PTI = Pretend to be ill and go home
PWM = Play with myself under the desk
RDM = Read dirty mags in the toilet
SBB = Smoke behind the bike sheds
SCJ = Stealing a car and joy riding
SL  = Switch all the lockers around in 'A' corridor
SOQ = Skateboarding in the outer quad
```

WHAT WILL HAPPEN WHEN ADVERTISERS ARE FORCED TO TELL THE TRUTH?

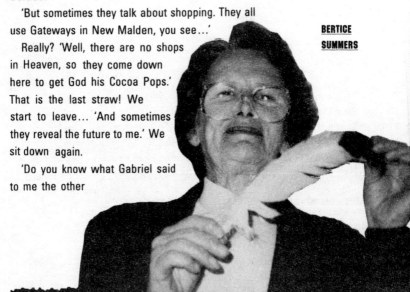

Bertice Summers is the only person in the world able to speak and to understand Enochian, the supposed language of the angels. As a result, angels apparently drop in for a chat any time they're in the area of Bertice's semi in New Malden. 'They bring little presents,' Bertice says, 'like manna and blessings, and new recordings by Jim Reeves and Bing Crosby.'

What does Mrs Summers say to her angelic visitors? 'I tell them to stop moulting feathers on my carpet!' she says. We *think* she's joking. 'Mostly, they talk about worshipping God. They say things like, "I'm bushed! I've just spent four millenia singing the praises of He who is above all. Got any lemonade, Bertice?"

'But sometimes they talk about shopping. They all use Gateways in New Malden, you see...'

Really? 'Well, there are no shops in Heaven, so they come down here to get God his Cocoa Pops.' That is the last straw! We start to leave... 'And sometimes they reveal the future to me.' We sit down again.

'Do you know what Gabriel said to me the other

BERTICE SUMMERS

day? He said "Bertice, save your string! There's going to be a string shortage soon!"'

We get up to leave again.

'"And Mike Lepine and Mark Leigh are going to come and visit you. They'll think you're a weird old bag."'

We sit down again. Maybe she knows something after all...

'"They'll want some ultra saucy prediction to spice up their unsavoury book, Bertice," he said. "Ho! Ho! Ho! I know some great ones, but unfortunately, I can't tell them to you because we don't have any of those words in Enochian. Instead, you are to tell them that their government is soon to pass a new law, requiring total honesty from all advertising in the future, no matter where it appears..."'

Sometimes you have to settle for what you can get...

BRITISH TELECOM COMMERCIAL

DIRECTOR: Sidney Gulliver

DURATION: 45 secs

(MAUREEN is dusting in the hall. The phone rings and she picks up the receiver)

MAUREEN: Hello?

CALLER: I know you... puff... gasp... I've seen you around. I want to pour whelks down your drawers...

MAUREEN: Ooh! Er!

CALLER: Do you know what I've got in my hand?

MAUREEN: The receiver?

CALLER: No. My...

(MAUREEN slams the receiver down)

MAUREEN: (To the receiver) You're a sick young man! I'm going to complain about you!

(MIX TO: MAUREEN later, on the telephone, looking exasperated)

MAUREEN: What do you mean, you won't do anything unless the police write to you promising to prosecute? Young man, only the Crown Prosecution Service can decide when to prosecute! The police can't give that undertaking... Yes, I do know that for a fact... Because my son is a solicitor, thank you very much... What you mean is, you won't help because it will put British Telecom out a little bit... With all your billions of profit, and you won't even help a poor woman who's... No, I won't shut up... And no, I won't pay £30 to change my number! Your service costs far too much as it is! Let me tell you, young man, I'm going elsewhere for my telephone service in future... Oh, oh yes... You are, are you... Well then, give me the home phone number of your managing director... Why?

(MAUREEN pauses and smiles to herself)

MAUREEN: Because I'm going to give him an obscene phone call he'll never forget!

VOICEOVER: British Telecom. We don't give a rat's arse.

BRITISH TELECOM COMMERCIAL

DIRECTOR: Sidney Gulliver

DURATION: 45 secs

(MAUREEN is knitting in her favourite armchair when her HUSBAND comes storming into the room waving a piece of paper. She is startled)

MAUREEN: Oy! (Clutching her heart and dropping her knitting)

HUSBAND: You stupid cow! I've just got the phone bill!

MAUREEN: And...? For that you storm in and rage and shout about?

HUSBAND: It's £700! For the quarter!

MAUREEN: Oh... (Visibly taken aback)

(HUSBAND crosses to MAUREEN and waves the bill angrily in front of her face)

HUSBAND: Use the Yellow Pages to do your shopping! Ring Cousin Milton in San Fransisco! Call our son, who's thirty-fucking-four and married, every single bloody night to make sure he's eating properly! Dial-A-Recipe Hotline! Yak, yak, yak to Mrs Furtleman

I'LL BET HE DRINKS
CARLING BLACK LABEL!

for hours on end - WHEN SHE ONLY LIVES NEXT DOOR! Accepting reverse charge peak rate calls from Great Uncle Mendel in New Zealand just so he can find out what the weather's like back home! Dialling the speaking clock every time anyone comes to visit just so you can prove how accurate your new gold watch is! YOU... STUPID... BITCH!!!

MAUREEN: (Resuming her knitting with ruffled dignity) Language!

HUSBAND: Well it's not going to happen again! Do you hear me?!

(HUSBAND crosses over to phone and rips it violently out of the wall, then runs to the window and flings the phone outside with all his might)

MAUREEN: There's still one in the bedroom.

HUSBAND: Not for long! (He rushes out of the room with a blood-curdling scream. We hear him pounding up the stairs followed by muffled loud bangs, crashes and curses)

(MAUREEN looks up, shiftily, at the ceiling, and then produces a cellular phone from under the cushion on her armchair and immediately starts dialling)

MAUREEN: Hello...? Mrs Furtleman? You'll never guess what's happened...

(FADE)

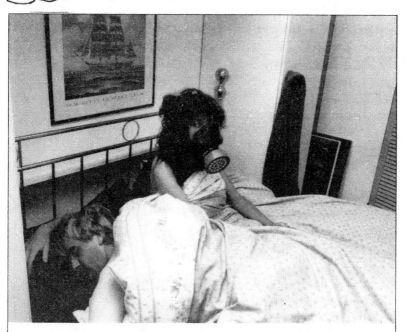

I'LL BET HE DRINKS CARLING BLACK LABEL!

MIDLAND BANK VECTOR COMMERCIAL

DIRECTOR: Barry Weinman

DURATION: 30 secs

(BOY talking to BANK MANAGER and ASSISTANT BANK MANAGER in office)

BOY: I want a new type of bank account.

MANAGER: (Patronisingly) Yes?

BOY: Yes, I want no bank charges.

ASSISTANT
MANAGER: (Patronisingly) No bank charges, eh?

THE NEW
DUREX
FEATHERLIGHT EXTRA

THE MOST EFFECTIVE FORM OF CONTRACEPTION YOU CAN BUY. BECAUSE, INEVITABLY, YOUR ORGAN WILL BECOME FLACCID THE MOMENT YOU TRY TO PUT ONE ON. AND AFTER HALF AN HOUR OF FRUSTRATION, SWEARING AND CURSING AND WASTING CONDOM AFTER CONDOM YOU'LL GIVE UP AND SETTLE FOR A HAND JOB INSTEAD.

IT MAKES YOU BURP

GOLDCREST
FAMILY SHAMPOO

You'll Like It. Fluffykins Didn't.

BOY: That's right, matey. And a cheque guarantee and cashpoint card.
            And no charges if I go into the red for a while.

MANAGER: Hmmmm!

BOY: And I don't put any money into it, but you give me, oh... let's
            say five hundred a month in there just to doss about with. And
            you give me a cheque book full of glossy colour pictures of
            Princess Diana in the nude. And any time I feel like it, I can
            just stroll in and get a tongue sarney from any of the girls
            on the counter, no questions asked. And alternate Saturdays...

MANAGER: (Cuffing BOY around the heard) Right! That's it! Fuck off,
            you idiotic little tic!

VOICEOVER: Here at Midland Bank, we'll listen to you... Until you start
            getting silly, that is. Then we'll ask you to leave.

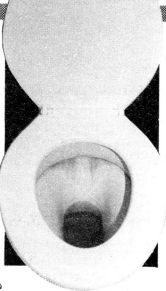

WE'LL TAKE THE CRAP FROM YOU

IF YOU TAKE THE CRAP FROM US

What do we mean?

We mean escalating charges, a poorly maintained Victorian sewer system, dangerous old lead piping, poor hygiene, routine dumping of toxins and waste on to your favourite holiday beach... and that's before we're privatised.

THE 10 WATER AND SEWAGE BUSINESSES OF ENGLAND AND WALES.

Everything you'd expect from a monopoly

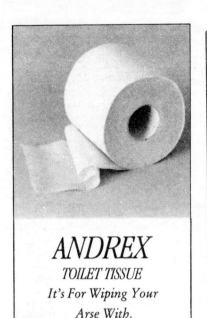

ANDREX
TOILET TISSUE
It's For Wiping Your

Arse With.

Divorcee, 34, three kids and serious mortgage difficulties, seeks anyone stupid enough to take this on in exchange for some unenthusiastic rumpy-pumpy and two hot meals a day. Box N16.

Nearly bald man, 48½, with considerable middle-age spread seeks quick jump. Photo appreciated, as I like masturbating over them when my mother goes out. Box N12.

Young vivacious blonde, 24, seeks lonely older man to give me lots of money and take me to fabulous places without getting anything in return. Box N89.

Beautiful, 25-year-old brunette, green eyes, is placing this advert with her mates as a giggle, just to see what kind of creeps and prats actually reply to these things. Box N4.

Psychopath, early forties wants your address and phone number so he can terrorise you. Box N30.

*It's Not Quite The Same When **HE** Eats One . . . Is It?*

For the very first time, political parties will have to tell the truth in their adverts and party political broadcasts.

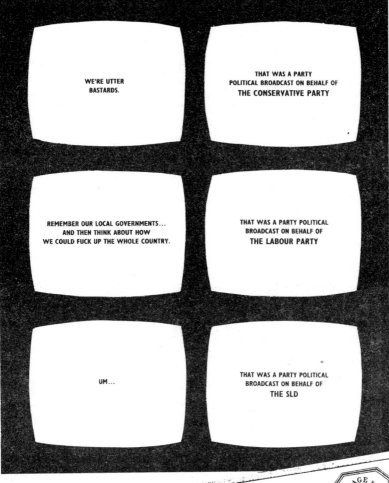

And junk mail...

THE AVERAGE LYING BASTARD GARAGE LTD

Date: 5 October 1994
Customer: Some stupid bird
Car: Ford with a koala hanging off the rear
            view mirror

£

Work undertaken (inc. parts)

		£
1.	Engine lubricant analysis and replenishment	25.00
2.	Hydro-scan evaluation	12.50
3.	Central automotive access attainment and phase one exploratory search	18.00
4.	Replacement of audial conducting unit	34.00
5.	Adjust electro-current throughput power inductors	48.00
6.	Replenish energy supply storage centre	27.50
Sub total		212.45
Labour: 7 hours @ £20/hour		180.00
TOTAL:		476.50
VAT @ 15%		112.68
SUM PAYABLE		657.8

KEY TO BILL

1 = change the oil
2 = check water level
3 = open bonnet and poke about a bit
4 = fix new aerial
5 = clean sparkplugs
6 = top up battery

Labour =

* 1 hour idly standing around listening to Radio 1
* 30 minutes taking car for burn-up around the block
* 15 minutes studying workshop calender and
  discussing Miss June and Miss November
  (and who would go the most)
* 35 minutes in toilet
* 50 minutes running hand over driver's seat and
  getting excited
* 5 minutes searching glove compartment for
  cassettes or anything else of value
* 30 minutes searching local breaker's yard for
  spares to pass off as new
* 30 minutes switching tyres for cheap remoulds
* 45 minutes looking for screwdriver accidentally
  dropped into engine
5 minutes getting replacement screwdriver from
workshop after fruitless search and repeated use
of the 'F' word
1 hour opening the driver's door after the little
plonker from YTS accidentally welded it shut
55 minutes replacing windscreen after 'Catch
the Spanner' got out of hand

DOLPHINS ARE REALLY STUPID BASTARDS!

That's the astounding claim made by celebrated East End psychic Mrs Betty Todd. She predicts that in the 1990s, for the first time, man will actually be able to *talk* to dolphins – only to discover it wasn't worth all the effort.

For, far from being highly intelligent creatures, Mrs Todd believes that dolphins are actually astonishingly thick.

'I saw it all in a vision,' she explains. 'Men in white laboratory coats standing by the side of a dolphinarium, talking to these two dolphins... and the dolphins were talking in English, but they were talking utter crap! They only wanted to talk about last night's episode of *Neighbours* and whether or not the scientists could arrange to have a few more gallons of Watney's poured in the tank.'

BETTY TODD

Dr Robert Fielding, professor of dolphinology at the University of Malibu, is astonished by Mrs Todd's claims.

'We are indeed on the verge of actually being able to talk to dolphins!' he confirmed. 'And more and more of my colleagues are rapidly coming around to the opinion that we would be better off talking to hamsters or career soldiers or really anything else in the animal or plant kingdoms. Dolphins, in my opinion, are not just stupid – they're ignorant.'

Dr Fielding believes he has already managed to decode some of the dolphin's whistling and clicking noises. 'They have favourite phrases, which they tend to use, ad nauseum,' he explains.

According to Dr Fielding, the most common are:

- 'I'll have you, you herring bastard!'
- 'Oh yeah? Make me, cod face!'
- 'There's plenty more fish in the sea'
- 'Oy, you human bastard, where's my fish?'
- 'God, I don't know what was in that scampi but it's done my bum in!'
- 'Yeeeeess! Mammory protuberances out for the lads, darlin'!'
- 'Kiss my spout-hole!'
- 'Still, you got to look on the bright side, haven't you?'
- 'When I was a kid I saw the QE2. It went right by me!'

Further evidence comes from a revolutionary Australian experiment, in which a team of scientists played classical music and simultaneously decoded the dolphins' speech patterns.

Here are their reactions, at first to Vivaldi's *Spring Concerto*:

DOLPHIN ONE:	Borrrrriiiing!
DOLPHIN TWO:	Poof music! Poof music! Mind your tails, lads!
DOLPHIN ONE:	Off! Off! Off! Off!
DOLPHIN THREE:	Come on, I'm off down the other end of the pool! You with me?
DOLPHIN TWO:	Yeah, all right. You got the ball?
DOLPHIN ONE:	Over here, son! On the head! On the head!
DOLPHIN THREE:	How about this for some tasty ball control?
DOLPHIN TWO:	Get out of it, ya flash bastard!

And now to Placido Domingo, performing *Woman is Fickle* from *Rigoletto*:

DOLPHIN TWO:	Gizzus the ball or I'll whack you straight in the bollocks!
DOLPHIN THREE:	Ah, you're crap! You're crap! I'm running rings 'round you!
DOLPHIN TWO:	Tackle!
DOLPHIN THREE:	Owww! You could have taken me bleedin' eye out!
DOLPHIN ONE:	Over here! On the head! On the head!
DOLPHIN TWO:	Wayhey! He goes round one, he goes round two… Goal! Goal! Oh yessss!
DOLPHIN ONE:	Come on, son! On the head! On the head!

So, sadly, it seems that Mrs Todd's prediction is not as far-fetched as it sounds. But it may be only part of the true problem.

Dr Lisa Gordon has spent over fifteen years alone in the Arctic, studying the song of the whale.

Far from being the hauntingly beautiful music of a highly intelligent creature lamenting its own evolutionary twilight, Dr Gordon is convinced that the song of the whales is actually a smutty little ditty.

'As soon as I realised what they were singing about, I packed my bags and came straight home to Tunbridge Wells,' says Dr Gordon, 'I say harpoon the lot of them!'

She is insistent that *nothing* has been lost in the following translation.

THE BALLAD OF MOBY'S DICK

We're the mighty sperm whales
— Errol Flynns of the sea!
So watch out on a Friday night!
Or when we take a pee!

Oh….
I got a big one, I got a big one, I got a big one, whoa!
I got a big one, I got a big one, I got a big one, oyyy!

It's bigger than a polar bear,
It's bigger than Nova Scotia
It's bigger than the dickhead over there
With the expensive sound recorder!

Oh….
I got a big one, I got a big one, I got a big one, whoa!
I got a big one, I got a big one, I got a big one, oyyy!

It drags along the ocean floor
Like some enormous anchor
Or floats up on the surface
Like a Liberian supertanker

Oh….
I got a big one, I got a big one, I got a big one, whoa!
I got a big one, I got a big one, I got a big one, oyyy!

(Repeat for quarter of an hour)

Scientific evidence has shown that whales are amongst the crudest mammals in existence.

So, maybe Mrs Todd has indeed seen into the future, and foreseen one of the twentieth century's greatest disappointments – successful communication with other species who, it just so happens, turn out to be cretins.

But why should this be? We asked Professor Murray of the British Oceanographers' Association for her opinions. Are dolphins (and whales) just 'no good'?

'No creature is born bad,' she explains, 'but, somehow, all the dolphins and whales seem to have undergone a cataclysmic mass trauma which has made them stupid – similar to that undergone by the human race with the advent of *The Benny Hill Show*.

'Clearly, the influence of the media is not at work here, so we must seek another answer. There are only two other things which are known to cause stupidity on such a huge scale and – since dolphins and whales have not been through the British comprehensive school system – I can only assume their moronic behaviour is due entirely to brain damage caused by all the toxic wastes we pump into the ocean.

'It's sad really, but this theory does at least help explain other puzzles, such as reports of seals reading Jackie Collins novels, shoals of fish who mysteriously congregate around the end of Brighton Pier whenever Cannon & Ball are down for the summer season... and, of course, the day-to-day behaviour of naval ratings.'

WILL THE QUEEN JOIN THE SUNSHINE COLA BEARS CLUB?

 One of the most astounding and, frankly, far-fetched predictions we heard while researching this book was that the Labour Party will win the next election.

But psychic Annie Stott is absolutely convinced. 'It's written in my mucous,' she tells us. You see, Annie has her own unique divination method: she sneezes into a tissue and then bases her predictions on what she finds there. This method sounds dubious to us, but apparently has been proven twice as reliable as Treasury forecasts, so who are we to scoff?

'When the Labour Party get back in,' she says, 'they'll be mightily pissed off about having had to spend so many years in opposition. The first thing they'll do is to take the Civil List allowances and reduce them to just 50p ... a decade. Well, the Monarchy will be in trouble straight away!

'The press will have a field day when the Monarchy are forced to sign on the dole. Millions will watch on TV as the Queen undergoes the humiliation of an interview at the local job centre in front of the cameras...'

ANNIE STOTT

INTERVIEWER:	I see, and you used to... rule?
THE QUEEN:	Yes.
INTERVIEWER:	And what exactly did that entail? Ruling, I mean?
THE QUEEN:	Um... Well, I'm not sure. One just had to be there, most of the time... One... one had to be on the stamps, I suppose. And opening things. I was good at opening things. Do you have any jobs where I could open things?
INTERVIEWER:	I'm afraid not, Your Majesty.
THE QUEEN:	Oh, that sounded nice! Say it again!
INTERVIEWER:	Your Majesty!
THE QUEEN:	Thank you, young man. Now, where was one? Ah, yes, I can Troop Colours...
INTERVIEWER:	Not much call for that, I'm afraid.
THE QUEEN:	I see. I know how to open Parliament... no? No. I see. Um... I know! Walkabouts! I could do walkabouts, collect bouquets of flowers, do a spot of waving to the crowd, that sort of thing.
INTERVIEWER:	I'm afraid we don't have anything like that on our books, Your Majesty. I've got some packing jobs in a factory...
THE QUEEN:	Packing? What does that entail, young man?
INTERVIEWER:	Well, sort of putting things into boxes.
THE QUEEN:	I'm sorry, I don't understand. Putting things into boxes? Isn't that what Harrods and Fortnum & Masons are for?
INTERVIEWER:	We'll forget that one.
THE QUEEN:	I know how to be Head of the Commonwealth...
INTERVIEWER:	Sorry.
THE QUEEN:	You don't have very many jobs here do you, young man?
INTERVIEWER:	McDonalds are always looking for new crew members...
THE QUEEN:	Oh, I wouldn't be any use to anyone on a boat. My son, Andrew...

INTERVIEWER:	No, You know, McDonalds! Hamburgers!
THE QUEEN:	I... I'm sorry. One is rather lost! Citizens of Hamburg? One shouldn't like to emigrate at one's time of life...
INTERVIEWER:	Why don't you just sign on next week as usual, Your Majesty?
THE QUEEN:	I could always knight people, I suppose...

Annie pauses to consult her tissue. We look away. 'I think that's a bear,' she says, puzzled. 'Don't you?'

Whatever you say, we tell her...

'As I see it... and the bogies never lie... just as the Monarchy start to hit skid row, along will come the multinational, Sunshine Cola Inc. – America's third largest cola company – with a unique sponsorship package. Coke and Pepsi have wrapped up the big pop stars – but neither of them has a monarch...

'And the Royal Family will have no choice but to accept. The first indications of the new-style Royal Family will come during the Queen's traditional Christmas speech in 1994...'

1.   INT.   DRAWING ROOM, SANDRINGHAM   DAY

THE QUEEN: Good afternoon. As Christmas approaches each year, one's thoughts turn increasingly towards the home and one's family and friends. Earlier this year, my family assembled at Glamis and we shall see a film of that auspicious occasion in a moment...

(QUEEN PRODUCES A CAN OF SUNSHINE COLA FROM BENEATH DESK)

THE QUEEN: ... But first, some yummy Sunshine Cola! It's one's absolute favourite taste sensation!

(QUEEN OPENS CAN AND TAKES A LONG DRINK)

THE QUEEN: MMMMMMM! This fizz is the bizz! If you have a right royal thirst, it's the King of Colas! And now, let us return to that misty morning at Glamis...

Annie foresees the Royal Family plummeting to even lower depths as the PR moguls from Sunshine Cola Inc. dream up more and more humiliating endorsements.

For example, the sentry boxes outside Buckingham Palace will look completely different...

As will the sentries...

And the accoutrements of state will fare no better...

The Royal Orb

The Crown

Sceptre

The Royal Coach

'And they won't stop there!' warns Annie. 'The Tower of London will be renamed "The Tower of Taste" and Sandringham "Sunshine Cola Mansion". Tourists will flock to see "The Trooping of the Cola".

'The awards in the New Year's Honours List will change radically. From 1995 onwards, people are rewarded for their services to the country by being made things like "Dame of the Taste Sensation" and "Knight of the Sunshine Cola Empire". And then, of course, there will be the multi-million dollar advertising campaign on television...'

SPRATT, DIGBY AND BERNSTEIN
ADVERTISING LTD

SUNSHINE COLA CAMPAIGN

CREATIVE PROPOSAL NUMBER 1

(The Queen, wearing her Royal robes, is rollerskating down a boardwalk. Skateboarding towards her is Prince Philip, wearing a conservative blue suit, kneepads and a crash helmet. He is clasping his hands behind his back as he skates)

A GIRL AND A GUY

(Close-up of Prince Philip as he spots the Queen. His eyes light up)

HE'S CATCHING HER EYE

(The Queen continues skating on. Prince Philip tries to impress her by doing some fancy skateboarding as he hurtles towards her. Cut to Queen's face. She is obviously amused.)

THE TIME IS RIGHT
IT'S A HOT SUMMER NIGHT

(Prince Philip skateboards past a hot dog stand. He skilfully snatches up a can of Sunshine Cola and flips the stand owner a coin)

WHEN YOUR MOUTH IS ALL DRY
THERE'S ONLY ONE DRINK TO BUY

(Prince Philip skateboards on with some more trick stunts as he approaches the Queen - who is still rollerskating serenely along)

JUST ONE SIP
ON YOUR LIP

(Prince Philip reaches the Queen and just when it looks like he's going to go straight past her, he swings around on a lamp post to change direction and stops right in front of her. He presents the Queen with the can and she gives him a nervous, girlish smile)

AND YOU'LL KNOW
SUNSHINE COLA IS HIP!

(Freezeframe on Queen drinking from can)

F.F.

But the biggest humiliation of all will be the bears that Annie spotted in her tissue: the Sunshine Cola Bears, that lovable gang of roly-poly little cola-obsessed funsters that are the trade mark of Sunshine Cola in America. The Queen will have to appear with them in cartoon adventures in children's comics...

Advertisement

Queen Elizabeth™
and the
Sunshine Cola Bears™

IN

'Pranks at the Palace!'

Boys! Behave yourselves! Oh no, my priceless vase!
I'm sorry, Your Majesty! Here, have this can of Sunshine Cola! It's my last, but I want you to have it!
Thank you, Bubbly Bear! Giving me your last can of Sunshine Cola means more to me than a gift from some smelly old Arab! You bears can stay!
Hooray! Three cheers for Queen Elizabeth!

... At book signings...

Her Majesty, Queen Elizabeth II, accompanied by those lovable little rascals, Bubbly Bear and Fizzy Bear, will be here in person at 2pm to sign copies of their new book

'The Mystery of the Stolen Cola Formula!'

... And during personal appearances and walkabouts.

WILL THE NINETIES SEE A NEW SEXUAL REVOLUTION?

'There's no doubt about it!' exclaims famous Wimbledon psychic Frank Jarvis. 'By the late 1990s everbody will be fed up to the back teeth with the 'New Morality' and 'The AIDS Scare' and there'll be a definite move towards gettin' 'em off and plunging into an out-and-out, shit-or-bust shag frenzy!'

Frank, who, it should be pointed out, is currently on probation for offences against his garden furniture, has had recurring dreams of a future in which every sexual deviation is indulged. He doesn't claim that these are genuine psychic visions, but he does like to talk about them at great length.

However, he firmly predicts that plans are *already underway* to provide a very special service to the forerunners of this new sexual revolution...

FRANK JARVIS

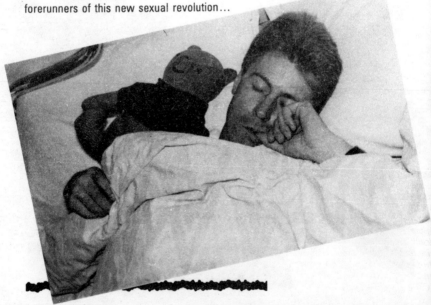

STRANGE? LONELY? OFFENSIVE? SHUNNED?

Then why not join

Perviedate

If you're a truly sick individual whose tastes are at odds with normal, decent society, we're just the thing you've been looking for!

No more lonely nights at home thinking, 'I'll bet the pet shop's closed by now' or gazing into window displays full of lingerie and wishing you had the courage to go inside and tell them it's for your identical twin sister.

No sir! Because now PERVIEDATE will FIX YOU UP with the fetish, perversion or outright obscenity of your choice, utilising the very latest in computer technology and the predictability of the male psyche.

So throw away your inhibitions and post the coupon today. You'll be glad you did!

CAN WE DELIVER?
JUST LISTEN TO SOME OF OUR WELL–AND–TRULY SATISFIED CUSTOMERS...

LAWRENCE AND DEBBI THE COURGETTE

I worked in a small regional tax office, where there was little or no chance to meet any courgettes. I used to see them on the supermarket shelves, of course, but could never pluck up enough courage to talk to them. So I turned to PERVIEDATE.

When I first saw Debbi, to be honest I thought she was a little on the plain side, but after I'd got her home and put the silk stocking on her and played some Sinatra, it all started to click.

My executive officer is looking for a tangerine, so I've recommended PERVIEDATE to him as well!

GARY AND HIS SKODA

Well, you see, I'm a masochist by nature, so I've always wanted a Skoda. Now, when I go out in it, I'm abused in droves by complete strangers. Everyone laughs and points at me and it feels sooo good that it's all I can do to prevent myself from ruining the upholstery. And when it keeps breaking down... well, it's even better than my old Fiat!

In fact, it's been such a great experience that I might come back to you in six months and get you to fix me up with a Yugo! Cheers, PERVIEDATE!

NORMAN AND PRINCESS

" *After Deirdre left me, I was lonely and depressed and thought I'd never find true love again. How wrong I was! Princess is all I could ask for in a partner – faithful, warm and obedient… and a right goer between the sheets! Now I understand why they say a dog is man's best friend!* "

Below, we've listed just a brief selection of the many thousands of exciting, dangerous and downright horrific perversions we can match you up with. Just tick your preferences, complete and return the application form and let PERVIEDATE get down to business!!!

You'll wonder how we did it, especially without being sick in the process!

YES! *I'm a pervert! And I don't care who knows it! (Well, I do; I mean, don't circulate my name on any lists or anything or send me back a big brown envelope with 'PERVIEDATE' stamped all over it or ring up my bank for a credit reference.)*

Please send me details of PERVIEDATE and show me how my squalid little fantasies can become an astonishing reality!

Name _____

Address _____

_____ Postcode_____

I would say I'm most attracted to the following (Tick three):

- ☐ Something involving Squaddies and large amounts of tinned peaches.
- ☐ Sweaty Rumanian gymnasts.
- ☐ Feeding my willie through a blender while someone plays opera music.
- ☐ Using the M25.
- ☐ Listening to Radio 2 (especially if Benny Green's on).
- ☐ Stockings and suspenders.
- ☐ Small, furry animals (with or without stockings and suspenders).
- ☐ Large, furry animals (with or without stockings and suspenders).
- ☐ Preferences developed in boys' boarding schools (with or without stockings and suspenders).
- ☐ Pure exhibitionism.
- ☐ Impure exhibitionism.
- ☐ Fruit and vegetables that would get a big laugh on *That's Life*.
- ☐ A short-sighted anteater with an exceptionally long tongue and an insatiable curiosity.
- ☐ Putting my bollocks between two big brass cymbals and performing the *1812 Overture*.
- ☐ Inflatable women with real hair and revolving tonsils.
- ☐ Musclemen who have this thing about septegenarian spinsters.

- ☐ Things that only MPs used to get away with.
- ☐ Being trapped in a lift with four Olympic-class weightlifters and a tub of Krona.
- ☐ Goings-on with a straightened-out paper clip that would make the Marquis De Sade flinch.
- ☐ I'm too ashamed to admit to liking this, but you know what I mean.
- ☐ Family-sized bars of Ex-lax.
- ☐ Making copies of my genitals with Play-Do and then leaving them in shopping malls.
- ☐ Anything involving Bovril.
- ☐ The cardboard tubes you get in the middle of toilet rolls.
- ☐ Licking lamposts late at night.
- ☐ Unpleasant things with drawing pins.
- ☐ Something so obscene it could never appear in print in any book which is going to be sold in W H Smiths.
- ☐ Something equally obscene, which you might just about get away with, but who wants to risk it?
- ☐ Islamic Fundamentalism.
- ☐ Especially ugly partners*
- ☐ A bathful of Copydex.
- ☐ Putting my private parts in a typewriter and hitting the 'X' key as hard as I can.

*If you ticked this box, you might find yourself better off going to Dateline.

INVENTIONS THAT WILL CHANGE YOUR LIFE

The Amazing Sabrina can tell you, in depth, just what sort of technological and social advances we will be experiencing in the 1990s.

Seen here with her owner, Mrs Mitchum of Potters Bar, with whom she communicates (exclusively), Sabrina will over the course of this book be our guide to some of the technological and social marvels coming your way in the 1990s.

**THE AMAZING
SABRINA**

There's a much more exciting future in store for the blind in the 1990s! For the first time ever, they'll be allowed to drive on Britain's roads – and, instead of being stuck with an insipid, wishy-washy labrador to guide them, they'll soon be offered a wide choice of more adventurous or unusual companions…

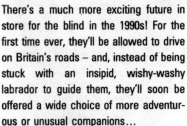

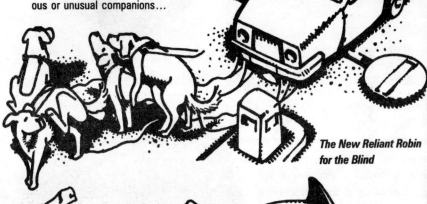

The New Reliant Robin for the Blind

The guide porpoise – for blind people who want to swim the Channel

The guide armchair – for blind people who are also violently agrophobic

The guide mole – for blind people who want to go potholing

The guide mollusc – for blind people who are quite happy to stay where they are

The guide giraffe – for blind people with a passion for the unusual

The guide orang-utan – for blind people who'd like to climb trees

The guide panther – for blind people who just want to show off

The guide bat – for blind people with an active sense of irony

The guide cod – for blind people who fancy a quick swim, followed by a tasty fry-up

The guide lemming – for blind people who are quite unable to come to terms with their disability

NAUGHTY CARS OF
THE FUTURE

 Psychic Mandy Foster told us that she sees the future by dancing topless in front of strange men. Sceptical of her claims we felt duty-bound to observe this phenomenon first-hand. Just to make sure her psychic abilities were genuine we repeated the observation. Mandy's vision was identical on seventy-eight different occasions.

Because of sleek, streamlined shapes and thrusting performance, women (and jealous men in Citroen 2CVs) have always claimed that men think of their cars as 'penis substitutes'.

Car manufacturers have always tried to capitalise on this to sell cars to sexually inadequate men. Mandy told us that this disturbing trend will reach its natural conclusion by the mid-1990s.

By this time manufacturers won't even bother trying to justify anything in terms of 'superior aerodynamics'; they'll just design cars that look exactly like penises.

By the end of 1996 Mandy foresees all the major motor manufacturers having at least one 'penis car' in their line up...

MANDY FOSTER

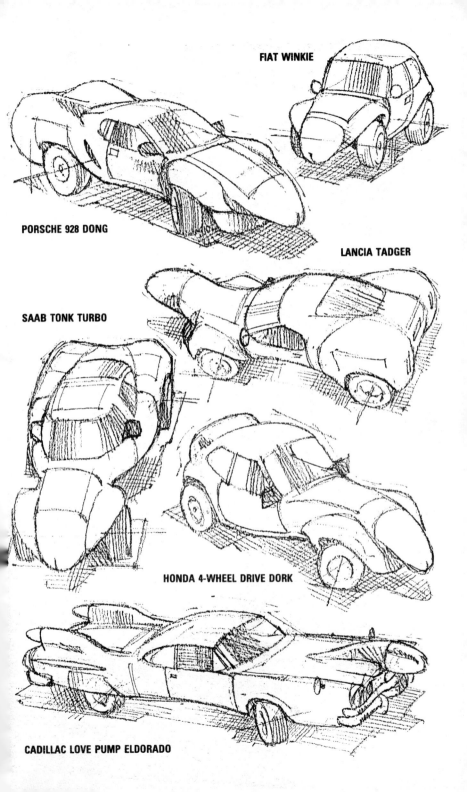

FIAT WINKIE

PORSCHE 928 DONG

LANCIA TADGER

SAAB TONK TURBO

HONDA 4-WHEEL DRIVE DORK

CADILLAC LOVE PUMP ELDORADO

BMW SERIES 5 'ERECTION'
Drive One Home Today

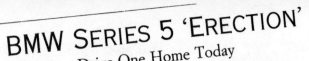

– Now Lead-Free For Cleaner Emissions!

THE NISSA
GLANS GLS

Be Cocksure About Your Car

AUDI COCK COUPE

Vorskin Durch Technik

THE LADA PRICK

Helps You Stand Out

From The Crowd

LADA WITHDRAW PRICK

It was recently announced that the Lada Prick will never reach Britain's roads. In wind tunnel tests at the Lada factory, the Prick revealed its inherent design fault at wind speeds of only 15 mph.

WIND TUNNEL TESTING THE LADA PRICK:

| *Wind speed 2 mph* | *Wind speed 10 mph* | *Wind speed 15 mph* | *Wind speed 25 mph* |

The £2 million advertising launch campaign, featuring Bernie Winters, Paul Daniels and Ian Botham with the slogans *'WEY, HEY! IT'S THE CAR FOR US!'*, *'YOU ARE WHAT YOU DRIVE'* and *'I LOVE MY LITTLE PRICK'* also had to be scrapped.

I LOVE MY LITTLE PRICK

SMALL ENOUGH TO SQUEEZE INTO TIGHT SPACES LARGE ENOUGH TO TAKE THE WHOLE FAMILY

They say that first impressions count. Well, when you first lay eyes on a Dick you'll be impressed. Just look at what the motoring press had to say after they road-tested it:

'As soon as I got a Dick in my hands, I didn't want to put it away.'

CAR WEEKLY

'You should have seen my neighbours' envious glances when they saw me washing my Dick in the driveway. Soon they were rubbing their hands over its smooth surface, inspecting it and asking for a ride.'

AUTO GAZETTE

'The Dick handled beautifully and was very responsive. A small nudge with your right foot and it would shoot off.'

MOTOR

THE NEW RENAULT DICK – WHAT'S YOURS CALLED?

As usual Skoda will get it completely wrong. Like other manufacturers, their research indicated that male drivers wanted cars directly resembling the male sex organs. They made the wrong assumption...

THE SKODA BOLLOX:

Does it Have the Balls to Succeed?

BY R. JAMES
MOTORING CORRESPONDENT

Skoda's long-awaited replacement for the aging Super Estelle was unveiled yesterday to a stunned crowd of motoring journalists.

This was to be Skoda's first entry into what has become known as the 'penis car' market – however, their radical design seemed to be the antithesis of the streamlined approach of their competitors.

Resembling a bloated pair of testicles, the car suffers from a drag co-efficient of 0.8, making it very unstable in high winds.

During a test drive at Brands Hatch I saw at least three Skoda Bollox keel over on a tight bend and then roll for several miles downhill before bouncing to a halt.

The testicular theme has been carried over to the exterior trim which has a pubic-hair like vinyl roof and what can only be described as a kind of 'spotty rippling' colour scheme.

With a top speed of 75 mph and only 25 mpg achievable in town, the new Skoda is certainly no winner in the performance stakes. Despite this, and its unconventional styling, if you're looking to spend about £4000 on a new car, there's still nothing to touch the Bollox.

Mandy foresees many owners of Renault Dicks and Lancia Tadgers with this in their rear windows.

MY OTHER CAR IS A DONG

Special car covers will also be available for the new vehicles.

WHAT WILL THE 1990s TEACH US ABOUT CHAIRMAN MAO'S TASTE IN SOCKS?

Robin Bennet is a heavy metal fan, but one who had an uncanny experience when he accidentally played Def Leppard's *Hysteria* album backwards after a night on the piss.

Not only did the album sound better, but a strange voice could be heard loud and clear above the music.

Being a typical heavy metal fan – and thus having nothing better to do with his life – Robin has transcribed the message, which turns out to be a glimpse into the future.

This was Robin's first psychic experience, although he did tell us that he once had a strange feeling that AC/DC were going to add an extra date to their UK tour – which they indeed did.

The message says that, after the handover of Hong Kong in 1997, China will really throw open its doors to the West. The best example of this will be the publication of certain thoughts of Mao Tse Tung that were originally censored and removed from the English language edition of his little red book...

ROBIN BENNETT

★ THE THOUGHTS OF CHAIRMAN MAO ★

I wonder if all penises have a bend in them?

I ought to buy some new socks. Grey ones would be nice.

Maybe I should change the wallpaper in my dining room.

I wonder what it's like to be a woman.

I wonder what it's like to shave.

Why does it always rain just after you've washed your bicycle?

Shall I have a rich tea or a gingernut?

I am convinced that one of my buttocks is bigger than the other one, but I am too embarrassed to ask anyone to check for me.

My bollocks are really itchy. I must see a specialist.

I must change my tailor. All my suits look like bundles of washing.

Those old Laurel & Hardy films really make me crack up.

Richard Nixon. What a cun

WILL MAN BE LIVING ON THE MOON IN THE 1990s?

'You can't keep a secret from a psychic,' says Wisconsin-based Mrs Renee Schwartz, talking to us in her living room in June 1989. 'I *know* that there are hundreds of people already living on the moon! And by the nineties there's going to be tens of thousands of them up there!

'You boys have been to New York and L.A. You know the cities are falling apart. There isn't adequate housing for all the inner city poor. So, if they're ever going to solve the problem, where are they going to put them?

'The moon, that's where…'

The moon. Right. We thank her for the coffee and brownies, silently thanking God that this trip has been fully tax-deductible, and make our excuses… And then she starts to get *horribly* convincing…

'Why do you think those *Saturn Five* rockets that went to the moon were so big? They were carrying all the materials required to build homes on the moon… and 200 low-income families each!

'Do you know why the space shuttle *Challenger* really blew up?'

We shake our heads.

'Because some stupid member of the Gomez family was freebasing in the cargo hold, that's why!' Mrs Schwartz crosses her arms in disgust. 'And why did *Apollo 13* never

RENEE SCHWARTZ

make it to the moon? Because the families had been sniffing the booster stage and using the fuel!

'You got this satellite TV in Europe, right. Sky TV. Have you ever seen it? Of course not, because it doesn't exist. They said they were launching a satellite, but really they were just shipping some more problem families. That's why Sky TV advertises such lousy programmes, employs people like Frank Bough and there's never a satellite dish in the shops when you want one. If anyone actually wanted to watch it they'd find it wasn't really there!'

Mrs Schwartz was becoming more convincing by the minute...

Are the families happy there?

This young gang member has customised his spacesuit. He will die in one-fifteenth of a second...

Spacesuits will be successfully adapted to carry on-board ghettoblasters.

'Not at all! They hate it! Especially the kids! Rather than being cooped up inside the moonbase with their parents, they spend all their time on the moon's surface, getting into all sorts of trouble...

Our next stop was to Kettering, where a school has been monitoring broadcasts from space since the days of Sputnik. One of the teachers, Mr Ron Willie, was intrigued by Mrs Schwartz's claims.

'We hear strange transmissions from the moon all the time. Just after the last shuttle launch, we picked up a transmission saying, "Cocksucker One, Cocksucker One, this is Pussy Station,

Mrs Schwartz's nightmare vision of the lunar ghettoes of tomorrow

Apart from junk food, the biggest criminal racket will be in bootleg cassettes of rap, hip-hop and salsa. Young people will steal, rob or even kill to raise the $2000 asking price for an L.L. Cool J album, which might be fourth, even fifth generation. However, these bootlegs will often be heavily contaminated and cut with other things and the death toll will be horrendous. A young tape-user might play a new Grandmaster Beastie Homeboy Posse tape on his suit-ghettoblaster, only to find himself listening to Rolf Harris or Tammy Wynette. He will panic, rip his helmet off and perish within two seconds…

In 1993, a twelve-year-old under the influence of the Rubettes will throw himself under the engines of a space shuttle and be burned to a cinder.

over"… I made the boys switch it off and do their prep instead.

'In fact, one of the strangest was when Apollo made its historic landing on the moon in July 1969. We thought then that the signals were being scrambled by a pirate radio station, so we never told the world what we'd heard.'

Here is a transcript of that historic transmission recorded by Kettering, published for the first time anywhere.

ARMSTRONG:	Houston, Tranquility base here. The Eagle has landed.
ALDRIN:	Hey, who opened the door?
ARMSTRONG:	Washington, get off that ladder!
WASHINGTON:	Hey, ah'm on th'moon! Fuck you! Fuck you!
MISSION CONTROL:	Hey, no Neil! You're supposed to say, 'That's one small step for man…'
ARMSTRONG:	Sorry, Houston. Junior Washington just got to be first guy on the moon instead, over.

MISSION CONTROL:	Oh shit, Eagle One. Get him back inside, over…
ARMSTRONG:	Washington, come back now, you bastard. I'm supposed to be the first man on the moon!
WASHINGTON:	Well tough shit, honkey mutha! Ah claim this here moon for all the black people, y'dig?
ARMSTRONG:	That's a big negative, Washington. Come back inside now and we'll pretend this never happened.
WASHINGTON:	Make me, asshole!
MISSION CONTROL:	What's going on up there, Eagle One?
HERNANDEZ:	Whut's all this shit 'bout claimin' the moon for the blacks? Washington, I come down there, I cut your black ass but good, *comprende?*
ARMSTRONG:	Buzz, stop him!
ALDRIN:	Too late, Neil!
ARMSTRONG:	Houston, that little runt Carlos Hernandez just got to be second man on the moon!
HERNANDEZ:	I claim this place for L.A. Warriors, man! It's turf now!
WASHINGTON:	Like shit!
ARMSTRONG:	Get back inside now, both of you!
HERNANDEZ:	You think you big tough astronaut hombre. You don' mean spit to Carlos Hernandez!
MRS HERNANDEZ:	You get back inside here *pronto, estupido*! I tan your hide! *Ventes aqui hijo! Vas estar muerto en uno moment! Tu es uno bastardo mas grande de tu padre!*
HERNANDEZ:	But Momma…!
MRS HERNANDEZ:	No buts… you let the nice Mr Armstrong be first man on the moon!
HERNANDEZ:	OK, Momma…
MRS WASHINGTON:	You hear that, Junior Bo'. Yo get yo ass in here or ah'll give you such a whuppin' you won't be sittin' for a week!

ARMSTRONG:	Listen to your mother, boy.
WASHINGTON:	Oh shit!
MRS WASHINGTON:	And mind yo' mouth, Junior! You want folks to think you wuz dragged up?
WASHINGTON:	Yes, Ma… Ah mean, no, Ma.
ARMSTRONG:	Thank you ladies… Mrs Brown… No! That's not the way to the bathroom!
MRS BROWN:	Well, silly me! I done got on the moon by mistake! Hey, look you can see th'Earth from here!
MISSION CONTROL:	Get her back inside, Eagle One. And we'll take this from the beginning all over again.
ARMSTRONG:	Buzz, give her baby a slap!… Mrs Brown, you'd better come in now, your baby's crying.
MRS BROWN:	You tell him Momma's comin'!
ALDRIN:	Welcome back, Mrs Brown. Quick, Neil, go for it!
ARMSTRONG:	I'm at the foot of the ladder now. The LM foot prints are only indented about 1–2 inches in very fine ground… Oh shit, Houston, I've forgotten what I'm supposed to say now, over.
MISSION CONTROL:	Get back up on the ladder, Neil, and we'll run it from the top. Over.
ARMSTRONG:	Oh yeah… Ahem!… Get back up on the ladder, Neil, over, and we'll run it from the top! Oh… Oh, sorry, Houston. Ahem, I'm back on the ladder again … Right… Ahem… Can you stop that baby crying, over… I can't hear myself think! Right… here goes. That's one small step for a man, one giant leap for mankind! Was that OK, Houston?
MISSION CONTROL:	Affirmative, Eagle One. We'll splice something together and release it to the world in a few hours. Houston, over and out.

Proof that mankind is already living on the moon, and will do so in ever-increasing numbers, just as Mrs Schwartz predicts? You must decide for yourself.

THE VAGINAL RUNWAY

A replacement sheet containing integral miniature LED landing lights, beacons and illuminated arrow symbols (mains powered), the 'Vaginal Runway' is designed to guide the male accurately towards the female during sexual intercourse in the dark, eliminating any chance of embarrassing fumbling, bruising or possible consummation of an illegal sex act...

A warning siren will sound if the male strays off the correct trajectory by more than five degrees.

DYING IN THE 1990s

There's no doubt about it! Old people are living longer than ever before, and this will have far reaching consequences for society. Extra strain will be put on hospitals, while demand for rheumatic bracelets, Sholleys, incontinence medicine and James Last records will reach unprecedented levels.

The area facing the greatest repercussions, however, is the funeral industry. Faced with a dearth in deaths, funeral parlours will find themselves up against much stiffer competition, so to speak.

And the one man who should know all about this is returnee from the dead, Arthur Cribbins.

Arthur died last year while under anaesthetic for a particularly nasty operation involving his private parts and a Hoover Turbopower vacuum cleaner. He claims that, while his spirit was in limbo, he met and had several long conversations with the dead, who gave him a fascinating insight into the near future.

It seems that, once a staid, sombre profession, undertaking will soon have to resort to aggressive marketing techniques to attract custom.

Arthur, who was successfully resuscitated by surgical staff (much to the annoyance of his hideously embarrassed wife Alice), described to us some of the methods that undertakers will use to drum-up custom in the 1990s...

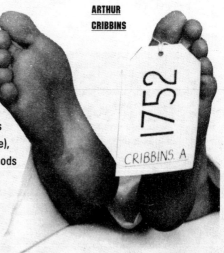

ARTHUR CRIBBINS

1752

CRIBBINS. A

STIFFS Я US

ONCE IN A LIFETIME OFFER!

We are now able to offer an a la carte burial service for the incredible, never-to-be repeated price of only £49.95!!!

Price includes:
- Coffin (choice of tea chest, supermarket trolley or oil drum)
- Transport to cemetary (trailered behind our vintage Sinclair C5)
- Polystyrene headstone (twenty letters max.)
- Wake at MacDonalds (inc. free hats and streamers)

WE MAKE NO BONES ABOUT OUR CHEAP PRICES!

Call FREEFONE CADAVER for immediate attention.

D.I.Y. FUNERALS LIMITED

We supply the coffin – you dig the hole!

Free shovel with every order!

A bulk purchase for an anticipated air crash means we have many many second-hand coffins which are 'as new'. Ask for full details.

DIY Funerals Limited
The Arches, Camberwell Street, Liverpool L8

Save £££££££'s on every purchase (ask for details of our *'Pay Now, Die Later'* finance scheme!).

COLIN'S

CREMATORIUM

- Cremations to suit all budgets

- Price includes ashes in a presentation cake tin

- French bread, fresh rolls and pastries also available.

Colin's Crematorium
17, Shepherds Lane
Bristol.

(Adjacent to Colin's Bakery)

WHY NOT HOLD YOUR OWN TUPPERWARE COFFIN PARTY!

Yes, you could earn BIG MONEY by holding a Tupperware coffin party in your own home for friends with elderly or sick relatives!

They'll be eager to buy once they see our extensive range of airtight burial vessels – and you explain to them how our coffins are specially designed to help preserve loved ones from traditional enemies of the dead, such as mould, maggots, worms and oxygen cellular decay, which traditional coffins can't keep out!

Yes, have a great party – AND earn valuable commission!

We're in the Yellow Pages

SALE NOW ON MFI

A cancelled order for 5000 wardrobes means we can offer flat-pack self-assembly coffins for only **£29.99!**

Just look at the features:

- One size fits all

- Constructed from walnut-veneer faced chipboard (non fire-resistant, so ideal for cremations).

- All hardware included: handles, screws, wood glue and padded lining.

- Choice of self-adhesive 'name plate' labels: mum, dad, granny, gramps, the boss, Tiddles and Rover.

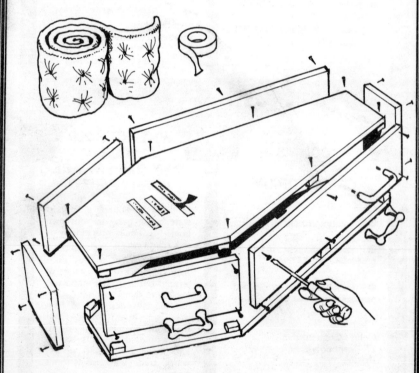

Complete with clear, concise instructions - so simple that even a child could make it! (If you want children to mess around with coffins, that is.)

Available from all branches of MFI.

KEEP YOUR MAN ON THE

STRAIGHT

AND **NARROW**

WITH HIS
VERY
OWN

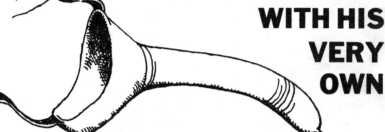

'PEE-PEE FUNNEL'™

Ugh! What's that vile smell in the toilet? Has the man in your life been spraying it about like a hosepipe again?

Isn't it embarrassing when friends or relatives discreetly say, 'God, do you know he's hosed down all four walls and your paper's starting to peel off? You really must do something!'

Now you can! With the new BRITISH DESIGNED AND BUILT 'Pee-Pee Funnel'™, he won't even be able to dribble on the porcelain, let alone dowse the lightbulb!

Safe, hygienic, one size fits all (except *really* pathetic ones).

Available now from all good chemists and women's centres.

THE MOST SUCCESSFUL TV COMEDY EVER

Colin Dexter can thank his local optician for his uncanny powers of clairvoyance.

'They gave me the wrong pair of spectacles,' he explains. 'In fact, they're so far off my regular prescription that all I can see through them is the future!

'I use the power sparingly, because the glasses give me a chronic headache and they look so stupid that I'm frequently mistaken for a train spotter or a virgin or both.'

What do Colin's magic spectacles show him of life in the 1990s?

'I was sitting watching 1994's television the other night,' he said, 'and on came their number one hit comedy show.

'Desperate for ideas, the BBC have obviously combined two of their biggest successes from the 1980s - *Yes Minister* and *The Young Ones* - to create a sure fire hit...'

COLIN
DEXTER

BBC

PISS OFF MINISTER AND SHOVE IT UP YOUR BUMHOLE

PILOT SCRIPT: EPISODE 1   "Who Dropped One in the House?"

Scene 1: JIM HACKER'S OFFICE. JIM HACKER IS PACING UP AND DOWN,
        LOOKING AGITATEDLY AT HIS WATCH. BERNARD WOOLEY STANDS
        NEARBY

JIM HACKER: Bloody hell, what's the matter with Humphrey? Our
                   think-tank meeting was meant to start hours ago
                   (snort).

(THERE IS A HUGE CRASH AS A BULLDOZER SMASHES THROUGH THE WALL OF THE
MINISTER'S STUDY, BRINGING DOWN PART OF THE CEILING. PLASTER AND DUST
ARE EVERYWHERE. HUMPHREY APPLEBY GETS OUT OF THE CAB)

HUMPHREY APPLEBY: Good morning Minister. Good morning hippy.

JIM: (Dusting himself down) And what do you call <u>this</u>,
                   matey?

HUMPHREY: It's a bulldozer: what do you think it is, you big
                   girlie?

JIM: I know what it is. What's it doing here in <u>my</u>
                   office?

HUMPHREY: It's in your office, Jim, because I drove it in here.

(CROSSES TO JIM'S DESK, PUSHES RUBBLE OFF AND SITS DOWN WITH HIS FEET
UP ON THE DESK)

JIM: Oh ha ha ha, Humphrey. That's very clever. A stupid
                   nerdy virgin like you would think that's really
                   funny. I suppose you think that ruining a cabinet
                   minister's office is a really adult thing to do.
                   Well it's not, matey.

BERNARD: Yeah, it's a cosmic bummer...

HUMPHREY: Shut up hippy! Actually, Jim, I got this bulldozer
                   to help shift the EEC butter mountain. I've already
                   started on the EEC lager moutain - hic - and I am
                   completely pissed. And yesterday I completely
                   cleared the EEC virgin mountain - except for you two
                   - by sleeping with 24,857 Swedish girlies in two
                   hours and it was completely brilliant and I bet you
                   wish you were there!

JIM: Aha! You're a liar! Sweden isn't even in the EEC!
                   So how do you explain that, smartie-pants? Ha ha ha
                   ha ha ha (snort).

HUMPHREY: Oh no! I have been taken advantage of by 24,857
                   girlies under false pretences (TURNS TO CAMERA),
                   some of them with quite enormous...

BERNARD: Actually, Humphrey, you were with me yesterday, don't you remember? We played Monopoly and you said it was in the rules that if you landed on my hotel in Mayfair, you could throw all my records out of the window.

JIM: Aha! So you are a virgin! (POINTING) Virgin! Virgin! Look over here everybody, there's a virgin in the Houses of Parliament, and his name's Humphrey Appleby!

(HUMPHREY GETS UP AND HEADBUTTS JIM IN THE FACE)

HUMPHREY: Now if you will excuse me for a moment... (Exits)

(SOUND OF CHAINSAW STARTING UP OUTSIDE DOOR)

HUMPHREY: (RE-ENTERS WITH CHAINSAW) I think it's time to reduce the EEC hippy mountain...

INVENTIONS THAT WILL CHANGE YOUR LIFE 4

BEFORE

THE TOJO
'BIG BOY'
HOLOGRAPHIC PENIS ENHANCER

AFTER

Invented, perhaps not without good reason, by the Japanese, this gold medallion and chunky ID bracelet you insist on wearing to bed is actually a cunningly disguised self-contained holographic projector which gives the impression of much greater endowment!

Watch them swoon, gasp, or hurriedly get their clothes on and run from the room, pausing only to stop and phone the *Guinness Book of Records*!

The miniature helium-cooled laser in the medallion will reflect a choice of ultra desirable 3D images off prisms in the bracelet right on to your penis.

Choose from Errol Flynn, Don Johnson, *'Shafty'* the donkey, Mike Lepine or Mark Leigh.

A severe paper shortage will blight the last part of the 1990s, giving rise to more thoughtful ways of using paper...

An example of how we'll be using paper more thoughtfully in the nineties

THE NIGHTMARE OF SELLAFIELD

'There are clues all about us now! Why won't anyone listen!' exclaims psychic magician Ali Rama from Manchester. 'Something terrible is going to happen around the Sellafield Nuclear Power Plant!

'You don't need to be a psychic! Last week, they found a turd the size of a car. It had been there for over a year before anyone realised it wasn't an abandoned Skoda, but the authorities still won't admit what radiation is doing to the area!'

Mr Rama gains his psychic insights by sending his astral body forward in time to actually witness events. He is now spending two years in 2090 for tax reasons but before he went, we asked him to travel to 1995 and see what life in Sellafield would really be like.

He came back with a handful of newspaper cuttings and a desperate urge to go to the toilet for a long time.

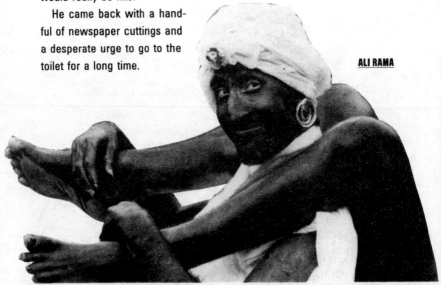

ALI RAMA

HERE'S LOOKING AT YOU KID!

Sellafield's annual Bonny Baby Contest proved as popular as ever with proud mums and dads this year. The show, as usual, was sponsored by Liverpool sick bag manufacturers, K T Witherspoon and Co.

And here are some of the proud winners!

▲ *Little chatterbox Jesus Christ What Is it Shipley, aged eighteen months, tied with himself for the Sunny Smiles prize. Lopsided Alan King, aged two, came second.*

▲ *Isn't he cute! Snorky Wayne Dudley, aged three years, who scooped the Baby With All its Limbs prize.*

▼ *Grunt Jackson, aged just five months, won the Evolutionary Throwback prize.*

OTHER WINNERS INCLUDED
Dwayne Kemp (Most Luminous Baby), Sharon Trent (Baby Most Resembling a Lozenge Award), Pukey Leon Sprat (Most Outstanding Ball of Pus in Human Form), Zapper George Smethurst (Baby Most Likely to Send a Geiger Counter off the Scale) and Nicola, Robin, Charles, Lucy, Jennifer, Michael, Kylie, Russell, Damian, Patrick and Tracey Dewhurst (Most Human Babies Sharing One Torso).

MY BUTTOCKS, MY ENEMY

Harry Stopes, 42, has called for his own buttocks to be arrested and taken into custody after they allegedly assaulted him on Thursday evening.

PERSONAL

MUTANT who shuns the light of day for fear of scaring children seeks warm tolerant male with poor sense of smell, 40–60. Box 35

NON SMOKING, attractive businessman, 38, 17 eyes, seeks woman with all limbs, for friendship, walks, dinners etc. Box 34

FED UP with men claiming they drive Porsches? Well, I am a Porsche (well, half Porsche, half Granada Ghia).
If you're looking to go places, I'm the sentient vehicle for you! Box 36

17 ACRES of prime Cumbrian countryside seeks similar. Box 37

LOST AND FOUND

Has anyone seen my budgerigar, Peter? He's blue, two years old and easily recognised by the fact that he's eight feet tall and a cyclops.
Small reward offered.
Tel: Sellafield 4303.

PROPERTIES FOR SALE

FOR SALE. Exceptionally large foxes' den.
Conveniently situated for earthworms, insects and small rodents. Would suit carnivore with small family.
Come to Farmer Digby's wheat field and shout.

WE ARE THE CHAMPIONS!

Sellafield once again scooped the jackpot in the Inter-Cumbria Fruit and Vegetable Growers Contest. Overall Winner was Mr Dennis Godley of Grange Farm, for his prizewinning two and a half mile long marrow (which answers to the name of Jonathan and can fly).

BIRTHS

MR AND MRS SMEDLEY would like to announce the birth of It! The Terror from Beyond Space (believed to be male). Weight at birth 8lb 4oz.

TO MR AND MRS GREENLY of Summerville Terrace. A healthy 6lb 4oz placenta, George Michael Greenly. Mother and afterbirth both doing well.

IS NEW TOWN HALL SENTIENT?

DEATHS

MR ALBERT JOHN RIDLEY, 65, departed this world by spontaneous combustion 5 April. Sadly missed by wife Winifred and sons Richard and Fido.

MRS GWEN DITCHWORTH, 45, departed this life 4 April, after a long and terrible struggle against a sentient lymph cancer which called itself Sidney. In memory, Peter and Jane.

IN MEMORY OF SIDNEY, a close personal relative. Died with his host, 4 April. Gone to be part of that great lingering illness in the sky. In memoriam, Larry and Sam Throat Cancer.

MR TERENCE WILLIAM BLETCHWORTH, 34, departed this world in a hail of police bullets after he unaccountably turned into a large, carnivorous slug in Tesco's last Friday. Rest in peace, Terry, love Mum.

IN LOVING MEMORY OF FLUFFY, devoted wife and mother, tragically devoured by a stoat April 3rd 1995. Sadly missed by Bobtail, Bunnikins, Hoppy, Fluffball, Snowy, Thumper, Fluffikins, Snowball, Furry, Fluffy Jnr, Downy, Whiskers, Carrot, Loppylugs, Patch, Twitchy and Trevor.

DEVOTED FATHER AND MOTHER, the much-loved a-sexual Jackie Merton passed away on April 4th. Survived in this life by four independently growing limbs, two buds and a wriggly mess on the bathroom floor.

NUCLEAR PLANT SAFE, SAYS CONTROLLER

There is no harmful radiation leaking from the Sellafield Nuclear Power Station, according to angry plant controller, *Stephen Appleton*.

In an exclusive interview with the *Sellafield Courier*, Mr Appleton, an extremely hirsute man, denied rumours that he was slowly turning into 'A kind of triangular human squirrel' and that his wife had recently given birth to 450 string sausages and a hedge.

Furthermore, he dismissed as ridiculous claims that a senior plant technician had grown to 400 feet high and had to be destroyed by army tanks as he blazed a luminous trail of destruction towards Manchester.

'Radiation levels in this area are not significantly different to those in the country as a whole,' he claimed. 'And all these wild stories of frogs claiming unemployment benefit and locals giving birth to things out of *Dr Who* are just stories made up by the *Sellafield Courier* to sell papers!'

He then terminated the interview by spontaneously combusting, along with twenty-seven other members of staff and the badger employed

WILL VICIOUS ALIEN ZYGOTES INVADE THE EARTH IN 1994?

'No,' says Belgian psychic Rene Ferriere emphatically.

'But you said they would on the phone!' we retort angrily. 'That's why we've come to Belgium to talk to you!'

'I misread my Tarot cards: the four of wands wasn't inverted after all... Sorry boys.'

'So, France won't be turned into one huge banqueting hall for the alien zygotes to dine at their leisure on millions of captive humans?'

'That's right. I think you should both be relieved!' says Rene petulantly.

'We're in Belgium for no good reason. That's nearly as bad!' We are not pleased.

'Don't you want to know what the cards were really warning us about?' Rene asks. 'You might as well. After all, what else are you going to do in Belgium on a wet Saturday night?'

We listen.

'The cards were really telling me that in the late 1990s manufacturers will be forced to reveal *exactly* what they've been putting in our food all these years...'

RENE FERRIERE

E213 Dried sewage
E418 The gritty bits you find when changing the sheets
E621 Thrush
E916 Scabs from a sore on a koala's bottom
E922 Pieces of toilet paper

E114 Alsatian night emissions
E387 Weeping pus from a third-degree burn
E413 Wildebeest spittle
E674 Hydrolised rabbit stools

E458 Water from the tank in the loft
E728 Concentrated bovine flatulence
E841 Bacteria

E383 Sugar concentrate
E749 Elephants' ovarian cysts

E117 Chimpanzee mucus
E150 The bits you find between your toes
E184 Putrefied haemorrhoids
E370 Varicose veins
E752 Marsupial pubic dandruff

GAMES OF THE FUTURE

Inside the world's computer networks is a vast and miraculous place where information lives, an almost infinite network of electrical impulses and other boring stuff that makes computers work.

Most people will never discover this hidden world because they've got much better things to do with their time, but for Kevin Tibbles, champion hacker and nerd par excellence, it is his playground, one where he won't get bullied or ridiculed, or throw up on the roundabout.

'You can go anywhere inside computers!' he exclaims. 'Last month I was trying to hack into Barclays, because I think banks can be very interesting places – not as interesting as building societies or marine insurance companies, but still interesting in their own right. I got the password wrong... and found myself in a very different place...

KEVIN TIBBLES

'I had accidentally stumbled upon the correct password for trans-temporal interfacing – and now I can hack into the 1990s!

'So now, when I'm not collecting the numbers of diesel locomotives or masturbating, I can play games from the future on my Spectrum computer! The trouble is, they're all utter crap!'

And he's right. They are...

THE TERROR AWAITING BRITAIN'S PENSIONERS!

 Gipsy Rose Rose is a clairvoyant with a very unimaginative and stupid name that provokes laughter in psychic circles.

Her vision, however, is nothing to laugh at.

We visit her in her gypsy caravan, on a piece of wasteland just off the North Circular Road, picking our way through jumbled piles of dirty, stolen car spares and discarded tyres, hordes of dirty, screaming urchins with no trousers on and dirty, vicious alsatians tethered by dirty rope.

'I apologise for the mess,' says Gypsy Rose Rose, beckoning us into her caravan, 'but we're a bloody, dirty, filthy, disgusting bunch of people.'

We cross her palm with £200 cash and sit down beside her. She tells us about her terrifying vision of the near future – a sinister government plot to kill off state pensioners because they're a drain on the country's resources.

'Don't you believe that Thatcher woman,' she tells us. We assure her that we don't, anyway. 'She just wants to punish everyone without a private pension plan.'

GYPSY ROSE ROSE

Gypsy Rose Rose spits in derision and makes the old Romany sign of contempt (sticking two fingers up and blowing a raspberry), and goes on to spell out, in uncanny detail, the whole evil plan. We are shocked.

... But not as shocked as we are when we get outside and find that our pockets have been picked.

Pensioners' Welfare in the 1990s
Your Questions Answered

PUBLISHED BY THE DEPARTMENT OF HEALTH AND SOCIAL SECURITY

Why is the name 'pensioner' or 'senior citizen' being replaced with the term 'parasitic scumbag'?
An unfortunate typing error. New guidelines in 2014 will set the record straight.

Why will I have to collect my pension from the Orkneys in future?
Centralisation.

I heard I could get supplementary benefit and extra heating allowance because I'm on a low income.
Well you heard wrong.

Why isn't it safe to walk the streets at night anymore?
It's your own fault – you're old, weak and feeble and remarkably easy to duff-up.

Why are we treated as second-class citizens?
Because you are second class.

Why did I work for fifty years and serve king and country for all this?
Life's a bitch...

Why is it no longer legal for two or more pensioners to congregate together in a public place?
To stop you blowing all your money on bingo.

I've heard that compulsory euthanasia might be introduced. What do you say to that?
We hadn't even thought about that one, but thanks for reminding us. We'll certainly consider it.

HMSO 35376/BH23/a

GOVERNMENT TIP SHEET No. 34
HOW TO KEEP WARM THIS WINTER

1. Jump up and down a lot.
2. Skin the cat and use its hide as a fur stole. (For additional warmth, soak your feet in a bucket of its steaming entrails.)
3. Burn your family albums, husbands' war decorations, letters from your children in New Zealand or Joe Loss records.
4. Urinate in a hot water bottle and take it to bed with you. (To avoid a build-up of dangerous gases, leave the stopper out.)
5. Keep your paraffin heater going all through the night, preferably in your bedroom. (For convenience, spare paraffin should be kept in buckets almost touching the heater.)
6. To warm water, place an electric blanket in your bath.
7. To retain the body heat lost through your head, try wearing a plastic bag over it.

HMSO 438/gf/45

In another sinister bid to shock and upset frail pensioners into an early grave, the government will publish a special magazine, and make sure it's delivered to every low-income pensioner.

x

Volume 1 Number 6 24 to 30 September 1992

THE PENSIONER

DISTRIBUTED FREE TO ALL PENSIONERS RELYING ON STATE HANDOUTS
- WHETHER THEY WANT IT OR NOT!

Our front cover illustration by W R Chumbly is of a Dalmatian pup being dismembered by 14 muscular, oiled negroes wearing scandalously little.

Contents

PROPRIETORS AND PUBLISHERS: *Her Majesty's Government, Downing Street, London W1.*
PRINTERS *HMSO Stationers, The Bridge, Park Royal, London.*
COVER *and editorial illustrations by Fuck! Ha, bet that caught you by surprise! Serves you right for being so idle that you have to read the small print for something to do in your meaningless existence. I'll bet you're a lonely widow too. Oh! What was that noise outside just then?*

Next Week's Issue

Features the *C word* where you'd least expect it, an extremely insulting article about the Royal Family, a gratuitous picture of excrement, we shoot the Lloyds Black Horse you're all so fond of, a distressing piece on dog-fighting, and full-colour pictures of an amputee kitten who's abandoned by its owners and accidentally wanders onto the M1!

Oh dear! We do seem to have trouble stopping our adorable little Jack Russell terriers from exploding these days, don't we! There goes *Skippy,* a faithful friend unaccountably blown to smithereens, taking his owner and two passersby with him. See ***Is Your Pet a Living Time Bomb?*** on page 160.

When Life is No Longer Worth Living

by Dame Celia Wilcroft-Ffipps

Yesterday, my shingles were playing me up dreadfully and I thought, 'You know, beyond sixty, life gets to be an intolerable burden.'

I mean, what do we really have to look forward to, except senile dementia, humiliating incontinence and being helplessly spoon-fed into a cold, dank twilight made hazy by almost unimaginable pain?

And then I thought, 'Buck your ideas up, gal! Show the fortitude expected of a Dame of the British Empire!' – and then I caught a glimpse of my hideous countenance in the parlour mirror, with its grizzled chicken neck like a relief map of Snowdonia, sagging Dali-esque bosoms and legs that looked like they truly belonged to something from the pleistocene era... Was *that* really me?

And then I thought, 'Fuck this for a game of soldiers! I'm going to stick my head in Cook's oven and hyperventilate!' But, of course, our precious North Sea gas is non-poisonous! 'I know,' I said to myself, 'I'll decapitate myself with the rotary mower, just like darling Amelia did when her servants found out about the colostomy bag!'

While I was debating this, what should drop through my letterbox but the new government brochure on euthanasia! Now, in three week's time,
(Continued on next page)

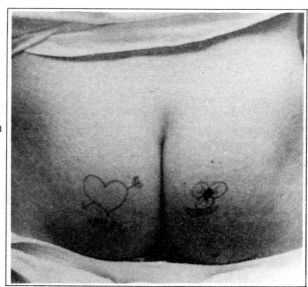

A big hairy, sweaty, workman's bottom which probably hasn't seen a soap and flannel since before decimalisation! But, oh, what unseemly passions and conflicts such a sight evokes!

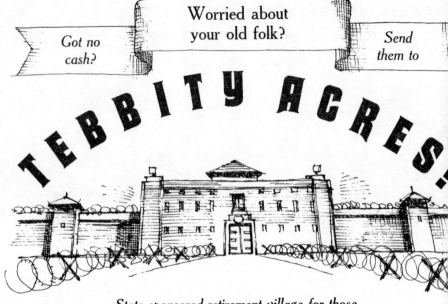

Worried about your old folk?

Got no cash?

Send them to

TEBBITY ACRES!

State sponsored retirement village for those without adequate private pension plans.

If you've got an elderly mother and father who aren't wealthy enough to retire to a luxury rest home or a bungalow by the sea, why not secure them a place at Tebbity Acres!

Set in fourteen square acres of partially redeveloped Merseyside warehouses in a prime riverside location, Tebbity Acres will ensure that your old folk have a productive life... proud that they are contributing to the State as opposed to being a burden!

Here's some answers to some of the questions we're most commonly asked about Tebbity Acres.

Is there plenty to do?

Of course! Every member is made to feel useful from dawn to dusk every day of the year, whether it's sewing up mailsacks, making licence plates, operating light machinery, or any one of the 101 other little tasks we subcontract!

Can we visit them?

Sadly, no. Statistics show that 95% of all pensioners die as a direct result of visits from close relations and, for their own safety, we regret personal visits and telephone calls cannot be entertained.

Well, can we write to them?

Of course, although pensioners in our care are not allowed to write back because of the unacceptable strain this might put upon their eyesight.

What's the food like?

Research shows that solid foods are bad for the elderly's teeth, gums and digestion. Therefore we offer a nutritious, well-balanced semi-liquid slurry three times a day which is perfectly adequate for their needs.

Will they be lonely?

Not a chance! We realise that loneliness *can* be a big problem for the elderly, so here at Tebbity Acres we house everyone in huge dormatories, with 175 retirees and at least 150 beds to each room. Lonely? Not on your nellie at Tebbity Acres!

Will they be allowed to handle their own money?

What money – they're poor, aren't they? No seriously, we believe it's best that the elderly are not taxed by financial concerns, so all State pensions and personal savings are ploughed back into the running of Tebbity Acres. Instead, we offer an incentive scheme, with little luxuries like toilet paper, soap and haemorrhoid cream awarded as prizes for good behaviour and successful completion of work duties.

Can they take their own personal possessions with them?

Personal possessions can create animosity and jealousy amongst the less well-off, so this is discouraged. We supply all our charges with free uniforms, bedding, a bucket and towel, which is all they really require.

Are the premises secure and will they be safe?

Absolutely 100%! We have a comprehensive, state-of-the-art analogue multiplex alarm system, CCTV, regular foot patrols, watchtowers, searchlights, four and a half miles of razorwire and Dobermann Pinschers just looking for an opportunity to kill someone!

TEBBITY ACRES
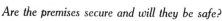
The future of the welfare state

A TERRIFYING TALE OF ALIEN ABDUCTION!

Jenny Machin has a fantastic story to tell. It's really a shame that it's got nothing to do with her prophecy so it can't be recounted here but, should you ever meet her, do ask her to tell it to you.

She also has a bizarre and, quite frankly, stupid tale to tell about being kidnapped by space aliens who showed her the future.

It's a story she tells with great conviction, pausing only to duck behind the sofa and consult a copy of Whitley Strieber's *Communion* where she thinks we can't see her.

'I was out driving late at night,' she recounts, 'when my car suddenly spluttered to a halt. Now, I drive a Skoda, so there was nothing unusual about this. But as I got out and lifted the bonnet up to see if the elastic band had perished, I became aware that I was not alone!

JENNY
MACHIN

'Standing in the hedgerow was a little bald man with gnarled, evil features and strange eyes. My first thought was, "What's Paul Daniels doing out here without his wig on?" The creature said something in an inhuman language that sounded like Welsh and then pointed a rod at me. I thought, "Great... He's come ten thousand light years just to flash me!"... but then the rod emitted a beam of powerful light which paralysed me!

'The next thing I know, I'm being floated on board a flying saucer and strapped to a medical examination table. Three of these little beings surrounded me and, finally, the leader spoke. (I knew he was the leader because the other two kissed his bottom before addressing him each time.)

'"We come from a planet in the Quark galaxy," he told me. "Our planet is dying, because we have had over twelve thousand years of Conservative government, and we are testing humans to see if we can live in peaceful coexistence with you.

'"We are extremely worried about the future of mankind. Your capacity for violence is terrifying and your stupidity unequalled throughout the galaxy. Only on Earth will you find pollution, war, famine, TV game shows and tabloid newspapers..."

'"And Strawberry Mivvis!" interjected his assistant, helpfully.

'"Yes, but they're all right." The leader seemed to get quite agitated. "The universe is not threatened by Strawberry Mivvis, is it?"

'"It could be. It could very well be, if you had a Strawberry Mivvi a hundred thousand light years long and it collapsed in upon itself under its own density and became a deadly 'Strawberry Hole', sucking in everything within its reach..."

'"But that's not going to happen, is it?"

'"It might ..." The assistant looked quite indignant.

'"Excuse me," the leader said. He turned away from me and vaporised what appeared to be his assistant's entire groin with a laser death blaster. "I'm sorry about that," he shouted, trying to be heard over the high-pitched screaming. "He hasn't been the same since he got hit on the cranium by that asteroid. Now where was I? Oh yes…"

'The leader then wheeled in a TV screen on which he said the future would appear, showing me the folly of mankind stockpiling nuclear weapons. Unfortunately, the set wasn't working properly and he couldn't seem to tune it in to that vision.

'Instead, the screen showed me the grim future for young couples trying to buy their first home. As I watched, it all became clear to me…

'Interest rates will continue to escalate, and even starter flats will be out of reach for ordinary people. Thousands will have nowhere to live, and estate agents will start going out of business in their hundreds…

'Finally, in their desperation, the estate agents will start trying to sell anything that people could possibly live in….

'The leader gave up, switched the set off and told me I might as well leave. He said they would return to visit me again and I started to lose conciousness. The next thing I knew I was back in my car.'

Have they been back?

'No,' says Jenny, 'although subsequently I did get a bill for £67.99 for the medical examination.'

Although absurd, Jenny's story does contain a recognisable element of truth. Estate agents are just the sort of bastards who would exploit the problems of the homeless for financial gain…

◀ *"I always wanted a home in the country" says first time buyer Joanne Jones, "And this hollowed-out tree is ideal!" The surveyor's report said there was no sign of Dutch Elm or Nottinghamshire Mank, so I snapped it up."*

Any problems?

"Just the neighbours," says Jo. "There's a squirrel's drey above me and they come in at all hours and toss their nuts about while I'm trying to sleep. Oh, and there's a bull in the corner of the field and I have to risk life and limb to go to work, or the cinema in town".

I did have a problem with squatters, but they were only chaffinches, so my boyfriend soon sent them packing".

▲ Bachelor Gary Todd thought he'd never be able to afford a place of his own on a salary of £20,000 a year, but now he's the proud owner of a cardboard box on the embankment.

'This is gentrifying very fast!' he says 'The police evicted the dossers who used to live here, and property developers moved in quickly to erect a row of upmarket cardboard boxes for professional people like myself. I paid just under £27,000 for the box on this site, with a 113-year lease!

'All the homes are subtly different, to avoid a boring uniformity. For example, I own a Tesco sugar carton, but the Christies next door live in a Heinz Baked Beans box. If you live at the posh end of the row, where boxes go for upwards of £70,000, you could be looking at a Moet et Chandon crate or even a Harrods food hall hamper!'

▶ It's a cheery wave from Peter and Jane Fletcher, who 'snapped-up' their Barrett's Starter Photo Booth in a 'flash' for just £45,000!

Conveniently situated by the Pic 'n Mix counter of Woolworths in Harrow, their home came fully furnished with a multi-level swivel-stool, curtains and mirror.

'We'd like to "develop" the property,' says Peter, 'principally by removing all those pictures of stupid grinning bastards with wanky seventies haircuts and tank-tops from our outside wall.'

▶ Richard and Jasmine Baker paid just under £70,000 for this very desirable rubbish skip within a stone's throw of London's Hyde Park.

'It's really spacious!' says Jasmine. 'We can both lie down in it and there's plenty of room to entertain guests. There are problems with fly tippers – Richard got struck on the head by someone dumping waste timber and had to have stitches, and I've been covered in leftover Chinese takeaways more times than I care to remember – but people are usually very kind and considerate.

'Right now, we're saving to buy a tarpaulin to drape over the top in inclement weather, but ultimately we'd like to buy a disused bottle bank within easy reach of shops and a station.'

◀ There's no place like home! And no one could be happier than newly wed Leslie Patterson and his beautiful bride Deirdre in their first home.

'It's not the home of our dreams,' admits Deirdre. 'In fact, it's just a public toilet in Lewisham High Street, but it is all ours! I've got a Baby Belling in there, and we take it in turns to sit down.

'My only fear is that one day I'll come home and find myself locked out, because I haven't got any 20p pieces!

'Under the terms of the lease, we have to allow members of the public to use it whenever they want to – which can be very distracting if you're trying to cook or watch a film or do the washing-up – but people are usually very polite and considerate and don't miss the porcelain or write graffiti on the wall paper.'

▶ *James Thorne paid just £16,500 for this* pied à terre *phone box in a swish part of Kensington.*

'It needed a lot of work on it,' he says, 'I had to get all the prostitutes' stickers off the window, and disinfect the accumulated years of piss staining the floor, but now it looks great!

'Privacy's a bit of a problem. Whenever my girlfriend and I started getting a bit amorous, we'd find the phone box surrounded by curious locals and Japanese tourists taking photographs and urging us to skip the foreplay, so now we always go back to her coalbunker.'

▼ *Retail manager Nicky Foster has never been late for work since he bought this sumptuous bench in Liverpool Street Station for a snip at under £12,000!*

'Who needs an alarm clock?' he grins. 'I'm woken every morning by the reassuring sounds of the station coming to life, dash to the toilets for a quick wash and brush-up and then the tube is just yards away!

'The neighbours are a great bunch. Ronnie down by platform eight is a quantity surveyor and the Robinsons in the waiting room have their own small business.

'The only drawback is that I'm repeatedly shat on by pigeons during the night.'

LUXURY HOMES IN ROYAL BUCKINGHAMSHIRE!

Saunders, Scumm & Bastard (U.K.) LTD.

(Incorporating CHEATE, SHYSTER, SWIZ & PARTNERS)

**ESTATE
AGENTS
OF REPUTE**

**RING:
(AMERSHAM)
45981**

**£24,999
Leasehold**

Ground floor maisonette. Immaculate one-bedroom dream home with
fitted headrests and ash trays. Plenty of storage space in dashboard!
Stones throw from main Chorley Wood road!

£19,950
Freehold for
quick sale

New instruction. We are sole agents for this one-bedroom home with
great potential. In need of some redecoration. Exciting, modern open
plan design. Easy access to all ammenities.

£29,999
Leasehold

Hurry! Attractive third-storey residence in much-sought-after
block! Includes all doors and axles! Private access from secret hand
and foot-holds.

Now You Can Afford A Home In The Home Counties!

JACKSON, JACKSON AND SPIV

EST 1988. Telephone: (Rickmansworth) 34290

CAR OWNERS! Thinking of dumping your old vehicle? Due to unprecedented demand we have hundreds of prospective clients seeking homes of all types. Estates and articulated lorries especially welcome. Free valuation without obligation.

First-time buyers get your skates on! Exciting, intimate one-seater starter homes in new apartment complex! * Curtains AND Ashtrays included with purchase * Some places still upholstered OR reclinable! Do yourself a favour and hurry now for rear or window seats!

Price: just £25,000 leasehold – 119-year lease!

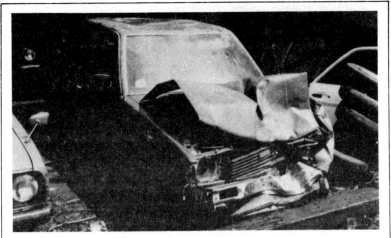

This could be the one you've been looking for! Superb, fully upholstered detached home with interesting dashboard and partial rear-view mirror!

* Close to main line station!
* Can't help falling in love with it!

Price £30,000 Freehold

★★★★★★★★★★★★★★★★★★★★★★★★★★★★★★★★★★★★★★

STAR HOME OF THE MONTH!

£45,000 Freehold!

Live like the Lord of the Manor! Unique opportunity to purchase this extravagant country mansion with wide frontage! * Huge, open-plan design with French window-style double doors at rear * Bonnet area converts into guestroom/granny flat! * Storage opportunities par excellence in exhaust pipe! * A dream home at a dream price!

★★★★★★★★★★★★★★★★★★★★★★★★★★★★★★★★★★★★★★

WHICH DAIRY PRODUCT WILL POSE THE GREATEST CHALLENGE TO CHRIS BONINGTON?

 1993 will be the fortieth anniversary of the conquest of Mount Everest. In commemoration, Chris Bonington, the world-famous British mountaineer, will set off on an equally challenging expedition. For the man who has climbed K2, the world's most difficult ascent, there is only one challenge left – the smaller, but equally treacherous, EEC cheese mountain.

Or so says psychic and hairdresser Georgie St Claire. Georgie told us about his recurring vision of Chris Bonington without any clothes on, but we put our fingers in our ears and went 'Whooo! Whooo! Whooo!' so he stopped and told us about the expedition instead.

According to Georgie, the EEC cheese mountain will consist of all the surplus cheese on the market after the lysteria scares of the late 1980s. It will be located about thirty miles north of Geneva, where it will remain perfectly preserved by the cool Swiss air...

GEORGIE
ST. CLAIRE

16 NOVEMBER 1992. In preparation for our historic ascent
we begin an intensive six-week training programme in
Sainsburys

IN TRAINING

Practising in the controlled environment of the
Sainsburys cold cabinet gives us a feel for traversing
cheesey surfaces

IN TRAINING

However, training conditions here are far from ideal;
we encounter frequent unexpected hazards such as impulse
buyers. Furthermore, two members of our expedition
become separated in the cakes and desserts aisle, and
mistakenly climb some cheesecake mix with varying degrees
of success

Fifteen minutes into the first day of our programme, our training comes to an abrupt end when Sainsburys' management expel us for 'being stupid'

Diary

JAN 25
In Geneva. Unfortunately some supplies have not arrived. Will
have to wait to decide whether to take advantage of the
present good weather or wait for more crackers.

JAN 27
Still insufficient crackers, but the decision is made for us.
Strong winds are expected shortly so decide to start climb at
the north-east face.

JAN 28
Establish base camp in sheltered hollow of Matured English
Cheddar. All team in good spirits about the task facing
us. Retire early after Welsh Rarebit dinner.

JAN 31
Team optimistic as the ascent progresses without incident.
Caerphilly gives way to Gruyere and Dutch Edam as we make
steady progress.

FEB 2
Bridle reports hearing strange sounds as we pass 2000 feet
altitude and others are aware of being watched. I cannot
detect anything untoward and put this down to hallucinations
from the strong cheesy smell.

FEB 4
Noticeable change in temperature as we reach 2800 feet. Smell
almost unbearable as we scramble up a crumbly slope of
Cheesy Wotsits, having chosen this ascent in preference to the
pile of savoury Cheese Niblets to the west.

FEB 10
Ascent difficult as the sun begins to make the cheese sweat and
become slippery. Barker also reports hearing noises, but

all I can detect is an eerie silence, broken only by the wind whistling through the Gorgonzola caverns.

FEB 13

We reach the top of the ridge and are greeted by a magnificent sight — a natural yoghurt lake in the bottom of a deep ravine of Camembert and Roquefort. Surely one of the seven wonders of the lactic world!

FEB 14

Awoken prematurely by Hutchinson who has discovered that our provisions have been ransacked. Broken TUC biscuits and Ritz crackers are scattered around our fire, and several jars of pickled onions have been smashed. It seems that whoever, or whatever, took them left the Crawford Flakey Biscuits — was it because its fingers were too big to remove the wrappers?

Team now distinctly uneasy. By dusk, reach a plateau of Stilton, broken only by scattered outcrops of Dairylea Triangles.

FEB 16

At 4600 feet. Bridle has found footprints in some Brie. They indicate the presence of a creature over nine feet tall. We have always dismissed the legends about the 'Abominable Mouse', known all over Europe by its various names — Monsieur Fromage', 'Cheesefoot', Die Ubermensch Teufelmaus' and Diablo Frommatore'. Could it be that it exists?

FEB 19

Tragedy! Brilliant sunshine has melted cheeses on the exposed upper slopes and we lost Taylor and Hutchinson in a ghastly Fondue avalanche — the very hazard we had been fearing most!

FEB 23

A Parmesan blizzard reached us in the early hours, reducing visibility to zero and making us crave for pizza, which we neglected to bring with us.

FEB 24

This cursed cheese! Storm finally over, however troubles continue. Two of the team, Bridle and Rogers, have come down with lysteria from close proximity to the soft French cheeses. We will have to delay our progress further until they recover from their sickness.

FEB 28

8250 feet and the summit is within reach. Noises heard again by all of us and a small cheeseslide delays our progress, but only a few hundred feet of spectacularly veined Danish Blue and success will be ours.

The diary ends there. In Georgie's vision it is found inside Chris Bonington's back-pack, floating on the surface of a cream cheese (with chives) flow just 250 feet from the summit. No trace of his body, or the other members of his expedition will be found. Georgie cannot see the events of that last tragic day. Perhaps the remaining expedition members succumbed to an excess of cholesterol, or plunged through a treacherously thin Kraft Cheese Slice; perhaps they fell victims to the Abominable Mouse. The truth lies somewhere in the cheese on that lonely summit...

A permanent monument, a cheese dish carved in bronze, will mark their brave attempt to conquer the EEC Cheese Mountain for Britain.

French Brie, the one cheese even experienced mountaineers fear (despite tasting quite nice)

Is this the footprint of the legendary 'Abominable Mouse'?

SEXUAL HARASSMENT IN THE 1990s

 The downturn in the economy will suddenly worsen in the 1990s, resulting in massive unemployment by the middle of the decade.

Psychic and unscrupulous boss Maurice Smithers-Maxwell foresees this having far-reaching (and advantageous) implications for those employers still in business. For the first time since the Victorian sweat shops, they will be able to pick and choose their workforce, giving sexually frustrated male managers the opportunity to employ the type of staff they've always wanted, but could never blatantly choose.

In one of Maurice's visions he saw the job application form of the future looking something like this:

MAURICE SMITHERS-MAXWELL

Application Form For Position of Accounts Clerk

PERSONAL DETAILS

1. Name _____

2. Sex: Male   [   ]   *If male, go to 3*
            Female [   ]   *If female, go to 4*

3. Fuck off

4. Age _____ *(if over 25, go to 5; if under 25, go to 6)*

5. Fuck off

6. Marital status: Married [   ]   *If married, go to 7*
                     Single   [   ]   *If single, go to 9*

7. Husband's job *(if applicable)*_____
(If truck driver, mechanic, policeman, rugby international, member of the armed forces or anything whatsoever to do with boxing, the martial arts or East End gangs, go to 8. If not, go to 9)

8. We are sorry but this job is far too menial for a lady of your vast talents and skill and suggest that you refrain from applying.

9. Address _____

_____

_____

(If this includes the words 'Womens Co-operative', go to 10. If not, go to 11)

10. Fuck off you lesbo.

11. Vital statistics: Bust____   Waist____   Hips____   Height____   Weight____
(Note: it is absolutely vital that this question is answered accurately)

12. Schools attended *(with dates):* _____

_____

13. Do you still have any of your uniforms by any chance?   Yes [   ]
                                                           No   [   ]

14. Did you get caned if you misbehaved?   Yes ·[   ]
                                                  No   [   ]

     If yes, did you secretly enjoy it?   Yes [   ]
                                                  No   [   ]

CURRENT EMPLOYMENT

15. Are you currently unemployed?   Yes [   ]   If yes, go to 16
                                          No   [   ]   If no, go to 17

16. Are you really, really desperate to get a job?   Yes [   ]
                                                           No   [   ]

    If yes, would you do anything to earn money?   Yes [   ]
                                                                        No   [   ]

    If yes, do you really mean ANYTHING?   Yes [   ]
                                                                No   [   ]

    If yes, would this include giving special favours
to the person who interviews you, no matter
how bizarre or repugnant these requests might
seem?   Yes [   ]
          No   [   ]

    (Now go to 20).

17. Name of current employer _____

18. Nature of current job _____
    (Now go to 20, or, if anything at all to do with feminism, go to 19)

19. Fuck off

20. Do you swallow?   Yes [   ]
                           No   [   ]

REFERENCES

Please give the names and addresses of two referees that we may contact:

a) _____   b) _____

   _____   _____

   _____   _____

(Special consideration will be given to applicants naming referees who have retired prematurely and who are now living in Homes For the Terminally Shagged.

Please send this completed form along with a photo of yourself (undressed) to:

      The Personnel Officer
      Acme Engineering Ltd
      62 Chandos Place
      Sunderland.

Lost For Words on 'The Morning After'?

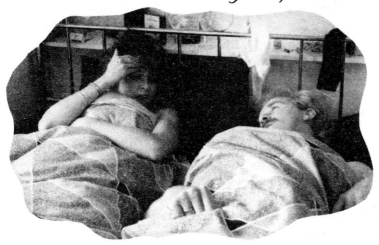

Now it's no problem, thanks to the

AUDIOTRON 2000

'Morning After' Prompter

This miniature, flesh-coloured capsule can be placed in the ear and when touched, secretly whispers to you one of twenty different suitable comments to make when you find yourself waking up next to a total stranger.

With the AUDIOTRON 2000, you need never resort to clumsy phrases like, 'Bollocks! I've slept in the wet patch', 'Fuck! I must have been really pissed' or, 'Aren't you Tony's missus?' in an effort to break the ice.

Don't Put Your Foot in Your Mouth - Put an Audiotron in Your Ear!

GOD'S GREATEST FEAR
FOR THE 1990s

 Nineteen-year-old Bobby Draycott doesn't claim to be a psychic. He's just a dedicated amateur radio buff... with an incredible secret.

We're sitting in his room at his parents' house in Ruislip, eating the peanut butter sandwiches and drinking the chocolate Nesquik his mother has brought up on a plastic 'Souvenir of Lanzarote' tea tray, when he decides to tell us his secret.

'I talk to God on my radio,' he says. 'No, seriously! Straight up I do.' He spots our disbelieving expressions and abusive hand gestures. 'Listen!'

Bobby goes over to his radio set and starts twiddling nobs furiously. We make a mental note that this might be good for a cheap joke later.

'Omnipotent–1, Omnipotent–1, this is Superstud, over...' Bobby leans closer to his microphone.

A moment of static and then: 'Superstud, this is Omnipotent–1. How are you, Bobby, over?' We are stunned. God sounds like Derek Jameson.

**BOBBY
DRAYCOTT**

'Not so bad, God. How are you keeping, over...'

'Mustn't grumble, Bobby. Your mum alright? Over...'

'Yes thanks. How's my granny, over...?

'She sends her love, mate. Over...'

'How's your son, over...?'

'Jesus? Oh, he's OK. Hurt his leg playing football yesterday, so he's hobbling around a bit at the moment. Serves him right. Over...'

'And Janice, over...'

'She's fine, Bobby. Over...'

'I hope you don't mind, God, but I've got Mike Lepine and Mark Leigh here and they want to speak to you, over...'

'Actually, I really want a word with them! Put the little toerags on, over...'

Terrified, we approach the microphone.

'I read your last book, you bastards! You're just lucky I'm not Allah! And don't fart when you're speaking to me! I hate it when I'm trying to talk to someone and they can't stop farting! Moses used to let rip whenever I appeared unto him. "Moses," I said, "you can just keep on wandering around the wilderness for forty years and shall never enter unto that place," I said, "because I'm not going to have you stinking out the Promised Land and spoiling it for whoever cometh after."'

'Er... sorry, God... over...'

'I'd save the frantic guffing for when you two find out where your eternal souls are going! You've spoiled Christmas! We used to have *nice* books, for genuine golfing enthusiasts, or full of pretty pictures of cats. Now it's all willies! I wish I'd never given you the bloody things. You misuse them anyway.'

The authors talk to god

'I've seen you, when you think no one's around! It's pathetic and disgusting! You could at least have a little consideration for the Omnipresent! And it's a sin, you know! It may not be in the ten commandments, but that's only because I didn't want *that* word in the Bible! Now I want you to stop doing it... and only write *nice* books in the future. Is that understood, over...?'

'Er... yes, God. Over...'

'Good! I like being obeyed! It reminds me of the good old days before all this "evolution" and "existentialist" rubbish came along. Now, what did you want to talk to me about? I'm very busy working in mysterious ways at the moment, so make it quick, over...'

And so we ask God what's going to happen in the 1990s.

And God told us.

Strangely, He didn't seem concerned about any major disaster or human tragedy (but then, He never has been).

Instead, He was far more concerned about the British Government's plan to deregulate the airwaves, so that anyone can start their own radio station, without needing permission.

'I live in the ether,' God explained, 'and it's soon going to be full of unpleasant and stupid broadcasts made by unpleasant and stupid people.' According to God, here are a few amateur radio stations you can look forward to…

Radio
DAVID PARKER
is a Moron
821-825m
The radio station that hates DAVID PARKER!

◀ ◁ ◀

RADIO REVERSE
848-850m
ALL THE HIT SOUNDS –
PLAYED BACKWARDS FOR NO GOOD REASON!

RADIO 'DAVID PARKER
IS NOT A MORON'
The radio station that defends DAVID PARKER, but really slags off that dickhead Les Southcombe (he's still a virgin, you know).

470-475m

Radio Turet's
Syndrome Piss Bollocks
Sufferers
264-ARSEHOLE-270 m
With shag shag weather bum forecasts, snot traffic updates shit hole, penis news on the wank bumhole hour, tosspot celebrity interviews and much, much more on-the-rag more!
Ringpiece.

Lose Your Lunch Every Saturday
at 2 with Ray Lumley's
'TALES OF THE GRATUITOUSLY GYNAECOLOGICAL'
only on RADIO RAY
228-230m

Radio Ghoul

— The radio station where you can win big cash prizes if we read out the name of your dead relative! Plus Extensive coverage of local traffic accidents, fires, terminal wards and tragedies!
195-198m

RADIO SUDBURY!
The only radio station devoted entirely to acrylic paint!
414-416 MhZ

We thank God for letting us know about all this and hastily make our excuses to leave, saying we have to catch our last train home.

'Oh no you don't!' God thunders. 'Being omniscient I know everything, *even* the London Regional Transport timetables, and your last train isn't until 11.45. Over…'

We agree to stay.

'I still haven't told you about the independent radio station that will really get on My tits (if I had any). Someone is going to pretend to be Me!'

According to God, the most offensive radio station on the air in the 1990s will be *Radio God* (West Midlands) and it will sound rather like this…

Hi there, mortals! God here and the time is just approaching 7.15. I'm looking down from heaven now and there's a five-mile tailback on the M6 northbound. On the good side I've supplied you with some great weather this morning so praise be unto Me and all that jazz!

> *Wake up every morning*
> *With a smile upon your face*
> *Because I am God, and God is here*
> *To save the human race!*

Now an old favourite from the Rolling Stones called *Get off of My Cloud*…

With this final message, there is an almighty rumbling through the speakers, a final crackle of static… and then silence.

God has gone.

We thank Bobby for his time and chocolate Nesquik, and walk to the station. It's only 11.30 – but the last train has left five minutes before.

God has stuffed us.

WHAT WILL THE CHILDREN OF TOMORROW BE LIKE?

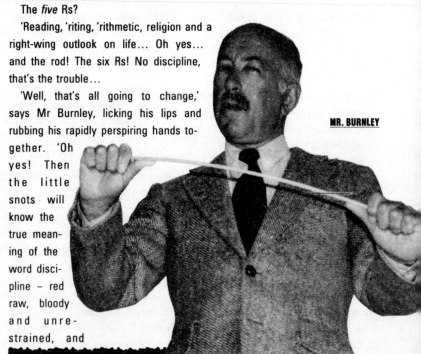

'A load of crap!' says Mr Burnley, a psychic who doesn't want his present whereabouts disclosed in case the people he used to babysit for in Milton Keynes read this book. 'Unless something is done about them soon, that is! Just look at this generation. I mean, they think Bros are good! When I was a kid, we used to play at something healthy, like war. Now they play at style. And do you know who I blame?

'The schools! They're too soft! They're too busy trying to teach kids how to be lesbians or socialists to instill any discipline into them. Whatever happened to teaching the five Rs?'

The *five* Rs?

'Reading, 'riting, 'rithmetic, religion and a right-wing outlook on life... Oh yes... and the rod! The six Rs! No discipline, that's the trouble...

'Well, that's all going to change,' says Mr Burnley, licking his lips and rubbing his rapidly perspiring hands together. 'Oh yes! Then the little snots will know the true meaning of the word discipline — red raw, bloody and unrestrained, and

MR. BURNLEY

woe betide the boy who cries for mercy! The army will seem like paradise to them then!'

According to Mr Burnley – who apparently gets his psychic visions by locking himself in the bathroom for long periods and making harsh, grunting sounds – discipline in schools is going to come back with a vengeance in the 1990s. By 1998, savage and violent punishments for even minor offences will become commonplace in schools..

For example, Mr Burnley predicts that pupils who talk in class will have their tongues ripped out and nailed to their lockers as a warning to others, and children found guilty of graffiti are likely to be crucified, naked and upside down, over a vat of boiling monkey poo for the entire duration of the summer holidays.

Thanks to Mr Burnley and his vivid predictions, we are able to picture life accurately in the classroom of 1998...

MONDAY MORNING

Period 1 in a typical London comprehensive

MR KEELER: Good morning boys. My name's Mr Keeler and I'm your new geography teacher.

SULLIVAN: WANKER!

(GENERAL LAUGHTER AND UPROAR)

MR KEELER: What did you say, boy?

SULLIVAN: I said,'Wanker', you wanker! What are you going to do about it, you.....AAAAAAAAAARGH! OHMYGODOHMYGODOHMYGOD!

MR KEELER: Right... Well... Is there anybody else who wants to lose an eye with a blunt instrument, or shall we get on with examining the eastern seaboard of the United States, as I believe Mr Nicholson was attempting last lesson?

SULLIVAN: AHHHHHHHHH! OHGODOHGODOHGODOHGOD... NOOOOO!

MR KEELER: Be quiet, Sullivan! The eastern seaboard is...

SULLIVAN: Oh God! Oh God! My eye!

MR KEELER: Right, come here... I said come here...

SULLIVAN: Yes sir... OOOOOOOOOOHHHHHHHHHH!

GRAHAME: He kicked Sullivan in the nuts!

MR KEELER:	Well observed, Grahame. Yes, I have indeed kicked Sullivan in the nuts... Would you like yours to be next? And Jenkins, stop being sick or I'll fuse your lips together with a soldering iron. Do I make myself clear, boy? Now the eastern seaboard is obviously dominated by what has become known as 'The Megalopolis', but one major city still dominates the region... Well, Richards?
RICHARDS:	Don't kill me! Don't kill me! I ain't done nothing!
MR KEELER:	Evidently...
RICHARDS:	*Our father, who art in heaven, hallowed be thy name... thy... unnnnnhhhhh!*
MR KEELER:	Right, who else hasn't done their homework? Salisbury? Reynard? Perhaps you'd also like to bleed profusely on the floor?
REYNARD:	No, sir... I mean, yes sir! I mean... New York, sir! New York, and its hinterland spreading back principally along the Hudson–Mohawk corridor, sir!
MR KEELER:	Very good... but your tie's crooked...
REYNARD:	AAAAAAAARRRRGUEEEECCCCCHHHHHH!
MR KEELER:	And you, Rigby. I don't like your haircut!
RIGBY:	EEEEEEEAAARGH!
MR KEELER:	Don't be a girl, Rigby. You can manage perfectly well with one kidney.
BENSON:	You're mad! You're stark raving bonkers! Well you ain't gettin' me!
	(PAUSE)
MR KEELER:	Well, is there anybody else who'd like to join Benson by jumping to his death through the classroom window? Or shall we recommence the lesson once more?

And where classroom discipline fails, the whole weight of the school will fall upon persistent offenders... ▶

Tedium et Bastardium

Harrow County School For Boys
The Drive
Harrow, Middlesex

21 October 1998

Dear Mr and Mrs Stott

I am afraid that, once again, I must write to you regarding your son's disgraceful behaviour.

He continues wilfully to disobey his teachers and do no homework. Furthermore, he is a persistent source of disruption in the classroom, where he seems to perceive himself as the class comedian.

Obviously he has learned nothing from his experience of being suspended by his thumbs from the main hall balcony as punishment for previous misbehaviour.

So it is my sad duty, as headmaster of this school, to inform you that as of 10.30 this morning I have signed the warrant for him to be put to death upon these premises on 1 November 1998.

If you would like to attend the execution, please complete the form supplied below and have your son hand it in to his year head.

Yours sincerely

J. Avery
Headmaster

....

I WILL/WILL NOT BE ATTENDING MY SON'S EXECUTION ON 1 NOVEMBER 1998

SIGNED ....

(Parent or legal guardian)

JS/867/21

....

An extract from the School Punishment
Book, Truro City Comprehensive,
May 1998.

NAME	PUNISHMENT	OFFENCE
Davenport P. (IR)	Finger severed	Stealing Chalk
Kirby S (2J)	Flogging	Being on fire during double maths
Jackson R (2J)	Flogging	Setting fire to Kirby S. during double maths
Thomas J. (4W)	Tarring and Feathering	Not playing as well as he could for the 4th year XI on saturday
Weinman L (3P)	Burying up to his neck in school sandpit	Forgetting homework
Burrie V (2D)	Flogging	white socks
Bowen S (5H)	Head shaved in front of assembled school	Trendy Haircut
Simpson O. (IR)	Having his genitals exposed for older boys to ridicule	Swearing in class
Farmer M 2P	Flogging	Forgetting Mr Davis birthday
Ebanks G (5W)	Columbian necktie	Staring longingly at Simpson O's genitals
Hamilton C (IL)	Kneecapping	Coming last in cross-country

Will the new punishments have a positive effect on pupils? Mr Burnley believes they will. In addition to consistently excellent academic results, he predicts a whole change in outlook amongst the young.

Indeed, by the turn of the century, were we to walk into any school toilets – and not get arrested in the process – this is the sort of graffiti we'd find…

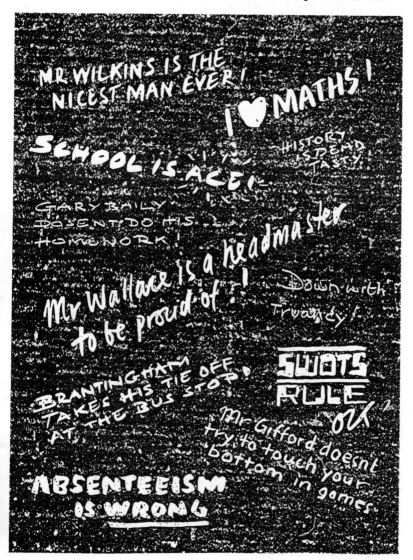

But what do today's top educationalists make of these predictions?

Professor Shafter, Head of Educational Policy Studies at Exeter University, told us, 'I think Mr Burnley is a very, very sick man with a lot of problems and you should tell the police everything you know about him.'

A NIGHTMARE FUTURE FOR BRITAIN'S BEERS

Eric Morris is a leading Northern clairvoyant whose psychic abilities are considerably heightened by twelve cans of Special Brew. At this point he collapses into what he calls a 'trance', his head full of strange visions.

Non-believers are frankly sceptical of Eric's abilities, especially since each trance is preceded by what he calls 'the traumatic side-effect of my Astral Self spanning the gap between now and the future' – violent vomiting and abusive behaviour.

Eric describes to us one of his most nightmarish glimpses of the future. In 1993, due to EEC Directive 1003/794/563A/4451/1 Section 13/2565/B75, *'Brand names of beers, ales and lagers must accurately reflect the principle contents therein'*. Here are some of the new brands that Eric, to his horror, foresees in the EEC's 'Brave New World' of the 1990s...

ERIC MORRIS

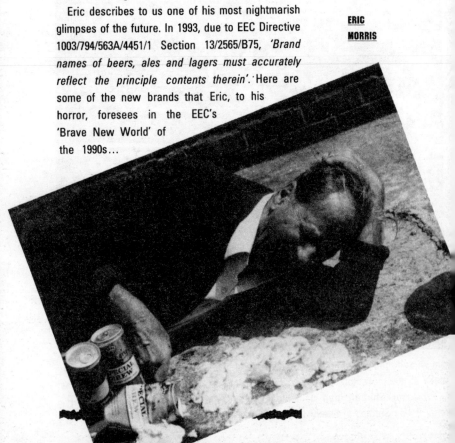

WAKEFIELD PREMIER

Sodium Monofluorophosphate

Halifax ZnSO₄ Old Poxy

with Nutras

ACCRINGTON'S OWN BEST HOPLESS

(Beer like your mother used to bring up)

TYNE & WEAR

BROWN ALE

(with added colourant)

Clitheroe Champion Pisse Water

TODAY'S SPECIALS

SALFORD FIZZY PECULIAR
KENDEL COUNTY EMULSIFIED
THRUXTONS CHEMICALLY IMPURE
GRIDDLESWAITE XXX CARBONATED
HUMBER BREWERY'S OLD FLOURIDE
WUZZOCKS ANTITOXIDANT E320
DARLINGTON STARCH-ENRICHED ALE
OLD AVON HYDROLISED BITTER
NOGIN RIBOFLAVIN
BARNSLEY OLDE ENGLAND EMETIC
MORECOMBE IMMATURE
(fermented in a cheap plastic
bucket for 2 days

THE SHOCKING SECRET OF THE ROYAL SUCCESSOR!

The Monarchy will be rocked by a major crisis, according to psychic Ken 'Baal' Smith of Surbiton. Ken is the chief of a coven of warlocks who meet regularly on dates of occult significance or if England are playing on the telly.

'Most of the time we just sit in front of the box with a few beers or go down the snooker hall. Occasionally we cast spells, but usually we're too busy helping each other repair the car, or there's a Clint Eastwood film on... But the other night, we did actually manage to summon up some demonic air elementals, who burst violently from our innermost beings. Sceptical members thought it was just the dodgy vindaloo we'd had, but I immediately fell into a trance and, when I woke up the next morning in Surbiton General, I realised the air elementals had granted me a vision of the future...'

It will all begin, Smith says, with the tragic death of Her Majesty in 1995 and the reading of her will...

KEN 'BAAL' SMITH

E718 ELL

Last Will and Testament

I, Queen Elizabeth II, being of sound mind and body (or of as sound a mind as any member of Royalty) do, upon my death, make the following provisions:

To my son, The Prince of Wales, Charles George Kevin Windsor, all the plants on the estates owned by the Crown, so that among them you might find the true love you've searched for all your life.

To my daughter-in-law, The Princess of Wales, Diana, the pile of women's magazines under the coffee table and the recipes I've been cutting out all these years.

To my grandchildren, Wills, Harry, Beatrice, Peter, Zara and Wayne, ten shillings each in premium bonds and any spare titles you can find lying around.

To my daughter-in-law, The Duchess of York, Sarah, my belly wheel and Jane Fonda work-out tape in the hope that, one day, you *will* be able to ride in the Royal Carriage.

To my sons, Prince Edward Henry Lionel Quentin Windsor and Prince Andrew Dickie John Thomas Windsor, you're both grave disappointments and you'll get nothing from me.

And to my most faithful companion, and devoted pet, Winston Cardigan Excalibur Virgil Anchor Beechwood Shortleg III, I do leave the United Kingdom of Great Britain and Northern Ireland and of my other Realms and Territories, my position as Head of the Commonwealth, the Royal Estates comprising Buckingham Palace, Sandringham, Balmoral, Glamis, Windsor Castle and all other properties, furnishings, monies, vehicles, etc., excluding those specified above.

Signed this day of *Eighth March Nineteen Hundred and Ninety Four*

by _____*Elisabeth R*_____

in the presence of ___*The Hon. Dennis Barker OBE*___

There will be immediate consternation and debate in Parliament as the country is rocked by a constitutional crisis of unprecedented proportions.

Edward Short	*(Dulwich East)* Mr Speaker, we simply cannot allow the Coronation to go ahead! The crowned head of Britain cannot be a *dog*! Having one as leader of Her... um... His... Its... Majesty's Government is bad enough!
Richard Johns	*(Tintagel)* May I point out the obvious advantages of a corgi assuming the throne! One, he won't bugger off skiing all the time. Two, the civil list can be slashed to include just Pedigree Chum, an occasional chew bone and some Bob Martin's tablets. Three, he won't upset people by going to some Nip bastard's funeral, condemning progressive architecture or shooting animals. Four, Prince Charles is completely bonkers anyway and Winston couldn't be any worse. Five, he isn't married to some vacuous airhead! Six, he has a far more...legitimate pedigree than our existing Royal Family and...
Margaret Thatcher	*(Finchley)* And, of course, seven, he will need the advice of his government in all aspects of foreign and domestic policy!
Neil Kinnock	*(Somewhere in Wales no one remembers)* So that's the Right Honourable Lady's plan, is it?
Margaret Thatcher	*(Finchley)* Shut up, Neil.
Neil Kinnock	*(Somewhere in Wales no one remembers)* Yes, ma'am.

From the pages of Hansard, the official Parliamentary record.

Oh King, you are
Snuffly and wet-nosed
Born to eat bones
Now you are king
How the fuck did
    that happen?

Poet Laureate Ted Hughes will magnificently capture the feelings of the whole British nation in a poem especially written to commemorate the Coronation:

Finally, as King Winston settles comfortably into his reign, a new national anthem will be composed in his honour, which will warm the hearts of true Britons everywhere...

◆◆◆◀

God bless King Winston
He's a very good boy
He'll come if you call him
Or if you wave his toy.

His coat is sleek and silky
There are no unsightly tufts
He's the first Royal since Princess Anne
To win a prize at Crufts.

His bark is gruff and manly
His haunches strong and sound
He doesn't curl up and lick his balls
If there's anyone around.

He likes his tummy tickled
He likes choc drops and fruit gums
And while he likes the other dogs
He doesn't sniff their bums.

He doesn't drool or dribble
He doesn't let off farts
He doesn't come right up to you
And smell your private parts.

He likes to go for 'walkies'
He sits up and he begs
He likes to meet young women
And have sex with their legs.

But he's on his best behaviour
With visiting Heads of State
He doesn't wrap around *their* legs
And vigorously masturbate.

◆◆◆

WILL THE '90s BE THE ERA OF 'THE CHILD GENIUS'?

 'If you look up my bottom, you can see into the future!' claims Southend psychic Jimmy McCabe. 'I call it my Time Tunnel.'

So, we don't bother talking to him any more. Instead, we travel to Putney, where psychic Kate Strachan lives.

'Somewhere or other – it might be America – they've proved that talking to babies while they're still in the womb or playing them music actually speeds up their development,' Kate tells us.

We sit enthralled. (Kate has a large cleavage.)

'Well, in the 1990s, they're going to perfect this technique and give rise to a whole generation of exceptionally bright little children. Little adults, in fact. And their progress will be very carefully monitored…'

KATE STRACHAN

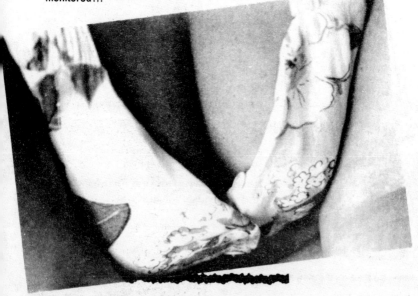

DAVEY 'CHEEKY CHOPS' KNIGHT

PROFESSION: FARMER

'When I took over this farm, it was losing over £10,000 per week,' says Davey. 'But, by taking a deliberately mixed approach to livestock in anticipating both arbitrary fluctuations in meat demand and seasonal requirements, I've taken us into the black!

'Now we have 500 head of moo-moos 200 baa-lambs, 200 piggies, 1000 intensively farmed cluck-clucks, two gee-gees and a dobbin... oh, and some quack-quacks on the south pond!'

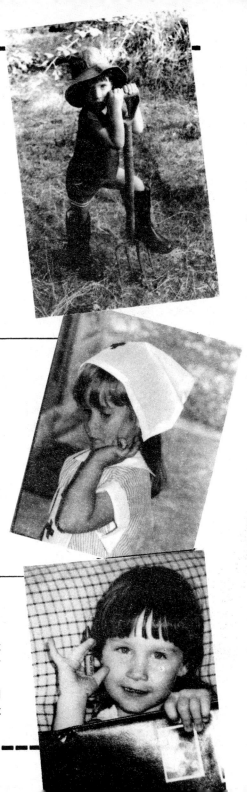

LEIGH 'CUTEY PIE' HIGGINS

PROFESSION: GYNAECOLOGIST

'Being so young has its definite drawbacks,' admits Leigh. 'No one will tell me what "that place" is called until I'm older, and when I protest, they just tell me to stop behaving like a proper little madam. So, I have to talk to patients about "Down there", "Your front bottom", "Number one hole", "Your rude place" and "Your woo-woo". Failing that, I just point...'

NIKKI 'SOPPY DATE' KING

PROFESSION: WRITER

Nikki is delighted because she's just been appointed as the new senior script editor on *Neighbours*.

'I have very little experience of real life,' she admits, 'but they tell me that won't be a drawback.'

BILL 'GRIZZLY GUTS' LESTER

PROFESSION: SENIOR MARKETING MANAGER, ICI CHEMICALS

'Senior management is a very challenging position,' says Bill, speaking from the office in his playpen where he keeps his phone, fax, PC and a panda called Norman, 'and I would be the first to admit that being under two is no advantage whatsoever! For example, I really resent having to go to bed before the six o'clock news – it affects my business acumen somewhat – and business lunches are a real hurdle. Very few decent restaurants serve Cow and Gate or rusks and I still haven't been properly potty trained yet, which can strain business relations severely!'

'Another problem is managing members of staff who are considerably older than me. Believe me, you don't get much respect when you have to wear your mittens on strings through your sleeves… Whenever I try and discipline someone, they just pinch my cheek and say something inane like "Who's a clever little boy then?"'

'Bastards.'

'Eventually, the technique's going to become commercially available,' predicts Kate, 'And everyone will be able to have "advanced" children. In fact, it won't be long before you can buy special workout tapes to play to your baby in the womb which will help them to grow up just like your favourite pop stars or film stars. Some, like the Meryl Streep and Pope John Paul II tapes will sell millions of copies…

'Others won't prove nearly so popular…'

'Some will actually prove dangerous,' warns Kate, 'and will rapidly be withdrawn from sale. The Arnold Schwarzenegger workout tape will be banned after women start trying to give birth to 4 stone 10 ounce babies, and the Kylie Minogue workout, after a horrifying side effect causes babies to be born with their brains missing.

'Despite these setbacks, the idea of "advanced" children will rapidly catch on and from then on, there'll be no stopping it!'

If Kate is right, by the end of the 1990s, the experience of giving birth will change almost beyond recognition...

SURGEON:	Push, Mrs Taylor, push! That's right! That's good!
BABY:	Oy! Get me out of here! This is just so gross! *(THIS IS JUST SO GROSS, GROSS, GROSS!)*
SURGEON:	Push... Push... Take a deeeeep breath, that's good...
MRS TAYLOR:	... My baby...
BABY:	Hello Mum *(HELLO MUM, MUM, MUM, MUM)*. Hey, nice echo in here! *(ECHO IN HERE, HERE, HERE)*. Hello... *(HELLO... HELLO... HELLO...)*. I wish I could yodel *(YODEL, YODEL, YODEL)*.
SURGEON:	Look, just shut up and let us get on with it. Push, Mrs Taylor... one... last...
BABY:	Owww! You got any sunglasses or anything? It's blinding out here!
SURGEON:	Congratulations, Mrs Taylor. You have a lovely baby boy!
MRS TAYLOR:	My baby!
BABY:	My name's Nathan.
MRS TAYLOR:	I wanted to call you Trevor, after your grandad...
NATHAN:	Thank God! Fresh air! After nine months of breathing that shit! So this is the outside world, eh? Not very big, is it?
SURGEON:	This is just the delivery room, now BE QUIET!
NATHAN:	Are you my mum? Bloody hell! And who's that dickhead over there with the video camera? Is that my

	dad? Oy, Dad, turn that thing off! I look disgusting – and who the hell will you show the video to anyway?
MR TAYLOR:	Sorry, Nathan.
NATHAN:	No… No… oh my God no! Don't! DON'T!
SURGEON:	Relax, Nathan. I'm just severing your umbilical cord!
NATHAN:	Oh… You mean that's not my winkie? This has come as a real disappointment!
SURGEON:	It's down there, Nathan…
NATHAN:	Jesus, have I been shortchanged!!! And get your hands off it, you bastard! It might break… God, do I have to resemble you two? I'll bet you're not rich either.
MR TAYLOR:	Nathan! You're not too young to be put over my knee and spanked, young man!
SURGEON:	Er… actually, he is…
MR TAYLOR:	Oh.
NATHAN:	Bloody hell! I've been out two minutes and you want to start mistreating me! And I'm dying for a fag!
SURGEON:	You *were* asked to quit, Mrs Taylor…
MRS TAYLOR:	I'm sorry, Doctor…
NATHAN:	And I'll get home and there'll be an el cheapo £3.99 Woolworth's teddy and a pukey coloured cot and pink blankets 'cos some cow of an auntie 'can always tell if it's going to be a boy or a girl', and a cheap mobile of rabbits and pixies that I'm supposed to find vastly amusing and entertaining, and some vomit-coloured, ill-fitting, woollen straightjacket that Granny has knitted because she's colourblind and fucking useless at knitting but no one's got the heart to tell her! Jesus H. Christ! No wonder babies cry!
MRS TAYLOR:	Doctor… um… I… I suppose it's too late to consider… um, you know… um… A–B–O–R–T–I–O–N?
NATHAN:	I can bloody spell as well, you know!

A somewhat exaggerated title in this case, we think. It certainly won't change *our* lives. At all. Not one iota. Nothing could be more irrelevant to us – in the entire universe – than new brands of lager aimed exclusively at the gay community.

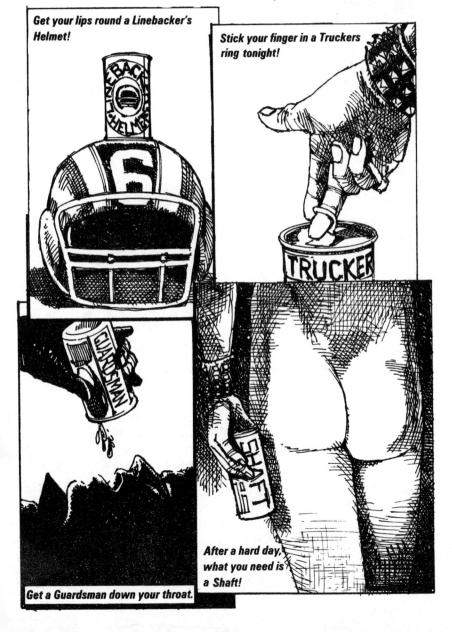

Get your lips round a Linebacker's Helmet!

Stick your finger in a Truckers ring tonight!

After a hard day, what you need is a Shaft!

Get a Guardsman down your throat.

HOW TO BEHAVE TOWARDS ROYALTY IN THE 1990s

'*Mystic Mary of the Rose*' (or Mary Piddlington, as she is known to the staff of the outpatients department at Milton Keynes Psychiatric) claims, 'I am the undisputed Witch Queen of all of Milton Keynes. Everyone is afraid of me! They give up their places in the queue at Waitrose when I come along because they know I could turn them into a... breadbin... with just a look! I'm good at breadbins. Do you see that souvenir tea tray from Weston-super-Mare? Mrs Beale from number 29! Horrible woman. I deliberately spill tea on her every night!

'And you're sitting on Trevor and Doreen who used to own the bakery. I really hated that woman. She used to put children in her buns, you know. So whenever I have one of my attacks of incontinence I make a special point of sitting in your chair, Mr Leigh.'

MYSTIC MARY OF THE ROSE

We shuffle, *very* uneasy in our chairs.

'Do you want to see my crystal ball?' she mutters.

Who did that used to be, we ask her.

She cackles again and starts to rummage in her drawers. (Actually, we mean the drawers of her sideboard but we couldn't resist a cheap joke.) She turns to us again, clutching one of those tacky souvenirs containing Tower Bridge, that you shake so it snows.

'From time to time, wondrous visions appear in my crystal ball!' she exclaims. Unfortunately this isn't one of those...

but if you complain I'll turn you both into toilet rolls.'

So we listen in silence.

One of Mystic Mary's recurring visions is that, by the late 1990s, respect for the Royal Family will have dropped to an all-time low – mainly due to their treatment by the tabloid press.*

Farquharson's Correct Form will swiftly be updated to reflect the universal lack of respect shown towards the Royals...

*In particular the *Sunday Sport* front cover of 3 October 1997: FAVOURITE ROYAL IN 3-IN-A-BED SEX ROMP

FARQUHARSON'S CORRECT FORM

Section 1:
ON MEETING MEMBERS OF THE ROYAL FAMILY

PERSONAGE BEING ADDRESSED	OLD PROTOCOL	NEW PROTOCOL
THE QUEEN	*Your Majesty* *Ma'am*	*Maj* *Queenie* *Oi! You on the stamps* *Mrs Windsor* *Liz* *Darlin'*
PRINCE PHILIP	*Your Grace*	*Phil! You old Greek bastard* *Wotcha, Phil! Shot any wildlife recently?* *Baldy*
PRINCE CHARLES	*Your Royal Highness*	*Charlie baby!* *Big ears* *Looney tune* *Chazza*

PRINCE ANDREW	*Your Royal Highness*	*Andy, How's tricks my old son? Still putting it about?* *Plonker* *Donker* *Mr Sausage himself* *Mr Rumpy-Pumpy* *Don't fancy yours, mate!*
THE DUCHESS OF YORK	*Ma'am* *Your Grace* *Your Royal Highness*	*Fatso* *Gingernut* *Fergie* *The Bottom* *Chunkers* *Sow features*
PRINCESS DIANA	*Your Royal Highness* *Ma'am*	*Di* *Darlin'* *Love*
THE QUEEN MOTHER	*Ma'am*	*Hello ducks! Come on:* *Knees up Mother Brown,* *Knees up Mother Brown,* *Under the table you must go,* *E-I-E-I-E-I-O*
PRINCE EDWARD	*Your Royal Highness*	*Eddie baby!* *The wet one*
PRINCESS ANNE	*Your Royal Highness*	*Horse face*
PRINCESS MICHAEL OF KENT	*Your Royal Highness*	*Sieg Heil!*

Section 2:
COPING WITH UNFORTUNATE SOCIAL INDISCRETIONS IN THE PRESENCE OF THE QUEEN

A) ON SUCCUMBING TO AN ATTACK OF FLATULENCE.

OLD PROTOCOL
'Please accept my humblest apologies, Your Majesty.'

NEW PROTOCOL
'Was that you, Liz? I didn't know you did things like that!'
'Cor! Phil! I told you to lay off the moussaka!'
'Those corgis – what a laugh, eh?'
'How's that for a right royal ripper?'

B) ON HAVING TO EXCUSE ONESELF TO THE LAVATORY.

OLD PROTOCOL
'Please excuse me, Ma'am.'

NEW PROTOCOL
'I can't hold it any longer, Queenie. Show me to your bog or you'll have piss all over the Royal carpet!'

C) ON NOTICING DURING THE TROOPING OF THE COLOUR THAT THE QUEEN'S HORSE HAS AN ERECTION.

OLD PROTOCOL
No comment is passed.

NEW PROTOCOL
'Jeez! Look at the shaft on that bastard. I wouldn't mind one of those – and neither would the wife!' (Followed by energetic pelvic thrusts)

D) ON HAVING ONE OF THE ROYAL CORGIS RUB HIMSELF UP AND DOWN YOUR LEG

OLD PROTOCOL
These dogs are certainly playful little chaps, Ma'am.' (Reach down to pat him and discreetly move him aside)

NEW PROTOCOL
(Shake leg forcefully) 'Gerroffff, you horny little tosser!'

E) ON NOTICING THAT YOU'RE USING THE WRONG CUTLERY AT A CIVIC OR SOCIETY FUNCTION.

OLD PROTOCOL
Put the incorrect items down and ask the head waiter to replace these with clean ones. Continue with the correct cutlery.

NEW PROTOCOL
Shout over to the most senior member of the Royal Family present – they're bound to know, e.g. 'Oi, Charlie! You've been to more of these dos than me. What spoon do I use for the quail's egg soup?'

F) ON FINDING THAT YOU'RE ACCIDENTALLY SITTING IN THE WRONG SEAT AT A DINNER TABLE OF A CIVIC OR STATE BANQUET.

OLD PROTOCOL
Offer profuse apologies to your host and the guest whose place you inadvertantly took. This should be followed up by an apology in writing.

NEW PROTOCOL
Explain the situation and ask everyone to stand up. Announce that you're all going to play an impromptu game of Musical Chairs; when the orchestra stops playing everyone should make a dash for their correct place. Anyone left standing must leave the banquet.

NEW HORRORS FROM AMERICAN TELEVISION!

Can you see into the future on your television set? Hundreds of people around the world claim to be receiving strange, unscheduled programmes on their sets in the early hours of the morning. And they could be watching tomorrow's television programmes! The good news is that no one has so far picked up a show with Anne Diamond in it.

How is it possible to receive TV from tomorrow? Some people think it's because television signals radiate into space at the speed of light. Eventually, they will hit a solid celestial body and then reflect back off it down to Earth again. But, because they have been travelling at light speed, they defy the laws of time and arrive back *before* they were even transmitted! Most people, however, think that the witnesses are just telling a pack of lies. They are wrong. Because we've actually seen the evidence: Mrs Corre Martinez of Culver City in Los Angeles has managed to video one of these 'television shows from the future'.

All we know is that the show proves just how out of hand America's passion for 'tabloid television' is going to get and that this show will be the nation's favourite at some point in the 1990s...

CORRIE MARTINEZ

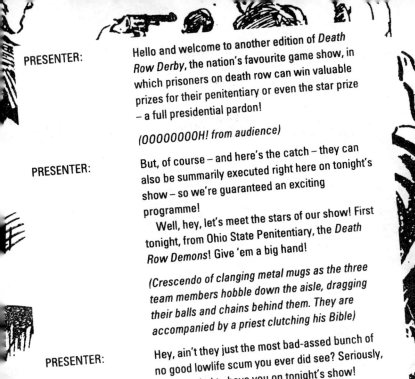

PRESENTER: Hello and welcome to another edition of *Death Row Derby*, the nation's favourite game show, in which prisoners on death row can win valuable prizes for their penitentiary or even the star prize – a full presidential pardon!

(OOOOOOOOH! from audience)

PRESENTER: But, of course – and here's the catch – they can also be summarily executed right here on tonight's show – so we're guaranteed an exciting programme!

Well, hey, let's meet the stars of our show! First tonight, from Ohio State Penitentiary, the *Death Row Demons*! Give 'em a big hand!

(Crescendo of clanging metal mugs as the three team members hobble down the aisle, dragging their balls and chains behind them. They are accompanied by a priest clutching his Bible)

PRESENTER: Hey, ain't they just the most bad-assed bunch of no good lowlife scum you ever did see? Seriously, hi boys, glad to have you on tonight's show!

KILLER JOE: Thanks Larry, we're pleased to be here...

PRESENTER: Great! Tell me, Killer Joe, what are you in for?

KILLER JOE: Multiple homicide, three states, kidnapping, trafficking in illicit substances and two counts of attempted homicide, Larry!

PRESENTER: And he's just twenty-two! Isn't that amazing, folks! A real big *Death Row Derby* round of applause for Killer Joe Kowalski!

(Furious banging of metal mugs)

PRESENTER: Now, their contestants tonight, all the way from California, let's have a big *Death Row Derby* welcome for... the *San Quentin Serial Killers*!

(The San Quentin Serial Killers hobble on)

PRESENTER: Let's just have a quick word with your captain. Bobby-Ray, I gather you're something of a celebrity!

BOBBY-RAY: Yeah, I'm the *San Diego Strangler*!

(Whistles and applause from the audience)

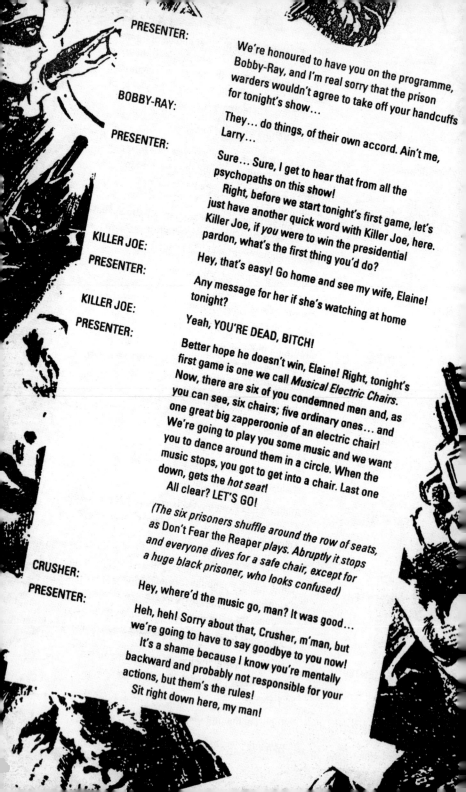

PRESENTER: We're honoured to have you on the programme, Bobby-Ray, and I'm real sorry that the prison warders wouldn't agree to take off your handcuffs for tonight's show...

BOBBY-RAY: They... do things, of their own accord. Ain't me, Larry...

PRESENTER: Sure... Sure, I get to hear that from all the psychopaths on this show! Right, before we start tonight's first game, let's just have another quick word with Killer Joe, here. Killer Joe, if *you* were to win the presidential pardon, what's the first thing you'd do?

KILLER JOE: Hey, that's easy! Go home and see my wife, Elaine!

PRESENTER: Any message for her if she's watching at home tonight?

KILLER JOE: Yeah, YOU'RE DEAD, BITCH!

PRESENTER: Better hope he doesn't win, Elaine! Right, tonight's first game is one we call *Musical Electric Chairs*. Now, there are six of you condemned men and, as you can see, six chairs; five ordinary ones... and one great big zapperoonie of an electric chair! We're going to play you some music and we want you to dance around them in a circle. When the music stops, you got to get into a chair. Last one down, gets the *hot seat!* All clear? LET'S GO!

(The six prisoners shuffle around the row of seats, as Don't Fear the Reaper plays. Abruptly it stops and everyone dives for a safe chair, except for a huge black prisoner, who looks confused)

CRUSHER: Hey, where'd the music go, man? It was good...

PRESENTER: Heh, heh! Sorry about that, Crusher, m'man, but we're going to have to say goodbye to you now! It's a shame because I know you're mentally backward and probably not responsible for your actions, but them's the rules! Sit right down here, my man!

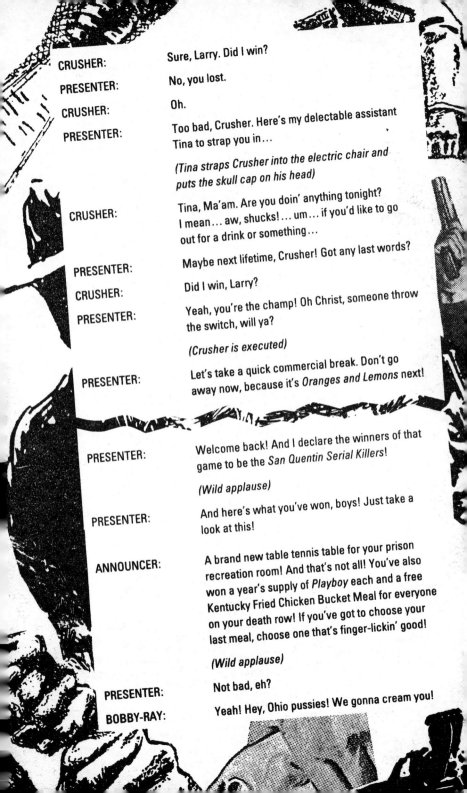

CRUSHER: Sure, Larry. Did I win?

PRESENTER: No, you lost.

CRUSHER: Oh.

PRESENTER: Too bad, Crusher. Here's my delectable assistant Tina to strap you in...

(Tina straps Crusher into the electric chair and puts the skull cap on his head)

CRUSHER: Tina, Ma'am. Are you doin' anything tonight? I mean... aw, shucks!... um... if you'd like to go out for a drink or something...

PRESENTER: Maybe next lifetime, Crusher! Got any last words?

CRUSHER: Did I win, Larry?

PRESENTER: Yeah, you're the champ! Oh Christ, someone throw the switch, will ya?

(Crusher is executed)

PRESENTER: Let's take a quick commercial break. Don't go away now, because it's *Oranges and Lemons* next!

PRESENTER: Welcome back! And I declare the winners of that game to be the *San Quentin Serial Killers*!

(Wild applause)

PRESENTER: And here's what you've won, boys! Just take a look at this!

ANNOUNCER: A brand new table tennis table for your prison recreation room! And that's not all! You've also won a year's supply of *Playboy* each and a free Kentucky Fried Chicken Bucket Meal for everyone on your death row! If you've got to choose your last meal, choose one that's finger-lickin' good!

(Wild applause)

PRESENTER: Not bad, eh?

BOBBY-RAY: Yeah! Hey, Ohio pussies! We gonna cream you!

KILLER JOE: Your mother, man!

PRESENTER: Ha! Ha! A bit of friendly rivalry here! That's what we like to see!

BOBBY-RAY: Hey man, I know where your kid goes to school … and these handcuffs can't stay on forever, man!

KILLER JOE: You touch my kid, you're history, pal!

PRESENTER: Whoa! Whoa! Whoa! It's just a game, guys! Right now, it's time to play *Oranges and Lemons*! Let's meet our celebrity axeman. He's someone I'm sure every criminal is terified of, Mr Vigilante himself … come in, Charles Bronson!

(Charles Bronson enters to thunderous applause, a large double-bladed axe slung nonchalantly over one shoulder. He shakes the presenter's hand

CHARLES BRONSON: Hi, Larry.

PRESENTER: Good to see you, Charles! Wiped out any street gangs recently?

CHARLES BRONSON: I was blowing away some lowlife on the Paramount set only yesterday, Larry…

PRESENTER: Ha! Ha! Great! Well, here's your chance to do it for real! Now you know the rules of the game. You and Tina form an arch with your arms and all the prisoners take it in turns to skip underneath it, while you chant that old nursery rhyme, but when the rhyme ends, you bring down your arms and whoever's trapped has to be beheaded, just like in the nursery rhyme!
All clear? Let's go!

(The prisoners skip underneath the arch, until the rhyme comes to an end, trapping a young white man with wild eyes)

PRESENTER: Sorry, Gerry, but you've got to leave us now! Sorry we never got a chance to talk. Gerry here specialised in killing children in a rather unusual way. Never mind… It's easier if you kneel down, Gerry!

GERRY: You ain't killing me man! You ain't killing me man! No! You ain't gonna do it!

KILLER JOE: Hey, you got a real chickenshit team, Bobby-Ray!

CHARLES BRONSON: *(Testing the weight of the axe)* It's different when you're the victim, isn't it Gerry? How many kids did you kill, you bastard?

GERRY: No! No!

(Gerry breaks free and dashes backstage. There is a fusillade of small-arms fire and then the unmistakeable rattle of a sub-machine gun)

PRESENTER: Thank you and goodnight, Gerry, I think! Thanks for being a good sport, Charles. Ladies and gentlemen, Mr Charles Bronson!

(Charles Bronson acknowledges the audience with a wave of the axe as he walks off)

PRESENTER: We'll be back after this commercial break... *Pass The Syringe* coming up next!

PRESENTER: Welcome back to part three of *Death Row Derby!* Gerry Peters from the *San Quentin Serial Killers* just departed this mortal coil in a hail of bullets! And here's what you've won!

ANNOUNCER: No more cold showers on your wing, boys! The new *Co-Zee Boilerheat* shower system will give you hot water whenever you want it! And it comes complete with a water softner to make your skin silky soft after your shower

(Wild applause from the audience)

KILLER JOE: I don't know about having silky soft skin with Big Billy Reynolds on the wing, Larry!

PRESENTER: Ha! Ha! Still, it's a great prize! Right, now it's time to play *Pass the Syringe*. Tina here is holding a syringe containing a lethal dose of cyanide. You cons pass it round clockwise until the music stops, and then the guy left holding it has to shoot up. All clear? LET'S GO!

(The condemned men start to pass the lethal syringe between themselves, to the accompanying sounds of Tie a Yellow Ribbon Round the Old Oak Tree. *It reaches Bobby-Ray...)*

BOBBY-RAY: Hey man, I can't pass it on! I got these handcuffs on! Take it from me, Killer Joe!

KILLER JOE: Shove it, m'man! The rule is you gotta pass it on!

BOBBY-RAY: I can't! Hurry man, the music gonna stop!

KILLER JOE: You were gonna get my kid, were you, asshole?

BOBBY-RAY: Shit! Shit! Shit! Shit!

PRESENTER: *(The music abruptly stops.)*

I guess that's what they call a *handicap*, Bobby-Ray! Ha! Ha! Seriously though, you've been a great contestant! Thanks for playing *Death Row Derby*!

BOBBY-RAY: Hey… hey, man! I can't shoot up! I've got my handcuffs on…

PRESENTER: Oh yeah…

BOBBY-RAY: *Perhaps if you took my handcuffs off…*

PRESENTER: Sorry, Bobby-Ray, you know we can't do that! Tina will administer the lethal injection for you.

BOBBY-RAY: Don't come near me with that thin… ahhhhhh!

(Bobby-Ray collapses onto the floor, kicks once and lies still)

PRESENTER: A big hand for Bobby-Ray, the San Diego Strangler!

(Wild applause)

PRESENTER: Guess it's safe to take the handcuffs off him now! Ha! Ha!

(The presenter produces a bunch of keys and, bending, unlocks the handcuffs. Instantly, Bobby-Ray leaps up, his hands around the presenter's throat in a vicious stranglehold. Killer Joe leaps forward and delivers a karate chop to Bobby-Ray's neck, killing him instantly.)

KILLER JOE: Hey man, don't you watch them movies? These psycho killers never die the first time you zap 'em!

Unfortunately, owing to some trans-astral interference, Corre's tape ran out at this point, so we won't know if Killer Joe wins his freedom or not for several years yet…

Stay tuned to this channel…

BOYS WILL BE BOYS!

Unless they're wearing the new

GELDATRON™
CHASTITY ENFORCER

Developed in close collaboration with
MOULINEX, GILLETTE, DURACELL and the **INSECT HOUSE**
at Regents Park Zoo, the **GELDATRON**™ will give your
boyfriend a thousand reasons to remain faithful –
twenty-four hours a day!

**Just take a look at some of its
highly advanced features!**

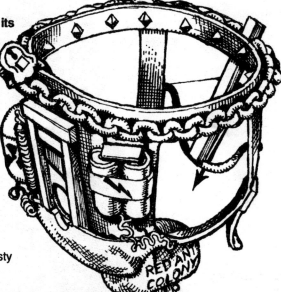

- One size fits all (except
  really pathetic ones)

- Completely escape proof

- Washable

- Sensitive to eight degrees
  elevation or above

- Hurts like hell

- Discourages that other nasty
  thing he does too

SO THE NEXT TIME YOUR MAN'S 'GOTTA DO
WHAT A MAN'S GOTTA DO', HE WON'T BE ABLE TO!

THE GELDATRON™ *CHASTITY ENFORCER*
Vorsprung Durch Aaaaaaaaarrgghhhhhh! Technich

THE SEARCH FOR THE ANTICHRIST

 This is Clive van Rothburg, the black sheep of the philanthropic van Rothburg family – a man who is secretly devoting his considerable fortune to lowering the quality of life in this country, and one of the prime suspects for the Antichrist predicted by Nostradamus, who will bring terror and destruction into the world in the 1990s.

Of all the potential Antichrists mentioned to us by psychics, van Rothburg has to be one of the likely candidates – rich, well-connected, supremely powerful and malicious, as we discovered when we researched his background.

CLIVE VAN ROTHBURG

Always anonymous, Clive van Rothburg has been the prime mover behind the all-too-familiar stories of misery and cruelty that blazed across the head-lines in the 1980s...

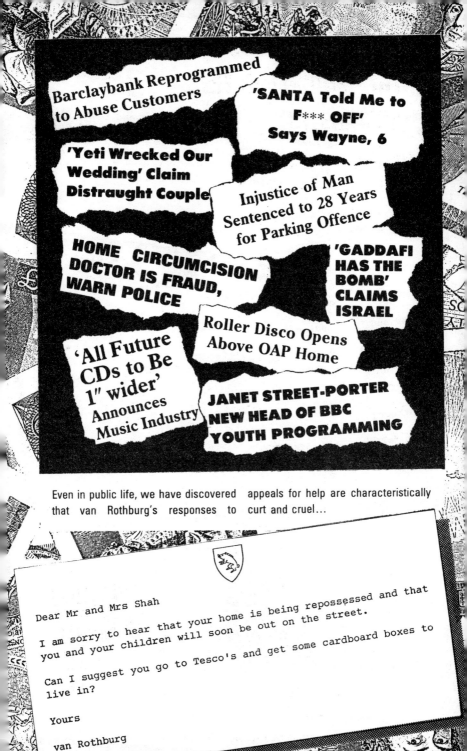

Barclaybank Reprogrammed to Abuse Customers

'SANTA Told Me to F* OFF' Says Wayne, 6**

'Yeti Wrecked Our Wedding' Claim Distraught Couple

Injustice of Man Sentenced to 28 Years for Parking Offence

HOME CIRCUMCISION DOCTOR IS FRAUD, WARN POLICE

'GADDAFI HAS THE BOMB' CLAIMS ISRAEL

Roller Disco Opens Above OAP Home

'All Future CDs to Be 1" wider' Announces Music Industry

JANET STREET-PORTER NEW HEAD OF BBC YOUTH PROGRAMMING

Even in public life, we have discovered that van Rothburg's responses to appeals for help are characteristically curt and cruel...

Dear Mr and Mrs Shah

I am sorry to hear that your home is being repossessed and that you and your children will soon be out on the street.

Can I suggest you go to Tesco's and get some cardboard boxes to live in?

Yours

van Rothburg

Dear Mr and Mrs Sugden

I was so saddened to hear that you can't meet your heating bills and are presently shivering in sub-zero temperatures.

In fact, I was so moved that I immediately shredded thousands and thousands of twenty-pound notes. I enclose the shreds herewith for you to burn in your grate.

Yours

van Rothburg

Dear Mr and Mrs Douglas

I was touched by your plight and a cheque for £500,000 is on its way under separate cover.

Yours

van Rothburg

PS I'm joking. Fuck off.

Dear Mr and Mrs Kettering

I was sorry to hear that you cannot afford to visit your son Keith's grave in the Falklands.

I was going to send you the return air fare, but have instead enclosed a nice drawing of the Argentinian flag.

Yours

van Rothburg

Dear Mr Winter

I was touched by your letter about your old, sick mother. My answers to your pleas are as follows:

a)   Tough shit
b)   That's your problem
c)   No
d)   So what?

Yours

van Rothburg

We have discovered that the massively misanthropic Clive van Rothburg is now making plans to immortalise himself and his misanthropic deeds – by building a permanent monument to his hatred and contempt for the world…

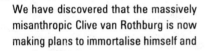

PUBLIC NOTICE

Notice is hereby given under the County Planning Act 1972 to erect a theme park of a size not to exceed 275,000 square acres on a site of (previously) great natural beauty.

Full plans have been submitted to, and are available for inspection at, the Civic Municipal Hall.

Objections, in writing, to the Town Planning Authority are a waste of time because the developer is a Freemason.

HALL OF UNSUNG HEROES
Life-like waxworks of some of the people who have helped make life just that little bit less bearable.
Meet:
– Mr F W Woolworth
– The world's first estate agent
– The writer of Agadoo
– The Ayatollah Khomeini's dad
Plus 3,000 PE teachers and 40,000 lawyers.

CRUELWORLD UNDER 10s AIR TRAFFIC CONTROL FUN CENTRE!
Calling all kids – take control of the crowded international airlanes with our very own 150,000 mW omni-frequency transmitter and totally misleading aircraft navigation beacon!
Play 'Chicken', 'Dodge'ems', 'Buddy Holly', and lots of other brilliant games!

MONKEY ISLAND
Incoming! Chimps under intense mortar fire! Try your skill, or just lob a few over because you feel like it!

INSECT HOUSE
Why not hire some big boots and go 'walkabout' in this open sanctuary? They're helpless... and crunchy!

I'VE SEEN THE LIONS OF SAFARI WORLD AND SHOT THE BASTARDS!

So is van Rothburg the Antichrist... or just another rich bastard? We'll soon find out...

'EASTENDERS' IN SPACE

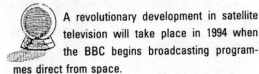 A revolutionary development in satellite television will take place in 1994 when the BBC begins broadcasting programmes direct from space.

This, according to top clairvoyant The Great Predicto, will be done in an effort to improve picture quality. In his vision the first live transmission will be the BBC's flagship, *EastEnders*.

The cast will be flown up to orbiting studios via the space shuttle to perform the show LIVE... although The Great Predicto says no one will anticipate how the conditions of zero-gravity will affect them...

THE GREAT PREDICTO

Exorcisms * Psychometry * Clairaudiance
Necromancy * Divination * Tarot * Palmistry

THE GREAT PREDICTO

24 hour service.

(No call-out fee)

Also, videos and televisions repaired at sensible prices.

EASTENDERS   Episode 1,352   Transmitted live 4 August 1994

Scene 1: INSIDE THE OLD VIC

Frank: Hey Pauline, can you work an extra shift for me
                tonight?

Pauline: That should be OK Frank, but I've got to... er... get
                ... um... back... I don't feel at all well...
                Bleuuurrrggghhhhh... to put Arthur's dinner in the...
                Bleuuurrrggghhhhh... oven.

Simon: I'll help out... Bleuuurrrggghhhhh... Frank.

Frank: That's good of yer Whicksy but I thought you...
                Bleuuurrrggghhhhh... had a date tonight.

Ethel: Oh no. My little Willy's floating in the air!

Sharon: Bleuuurrrggghhhhh...

Simon: I thought they told you to put lead shoes on him, like
                the rest of... Bleuuurrrggghhhhh... us.

Ethel: Bleuuurrrggghhhhh... I couldn't find any his size.

Arthur: (On entering pub) Bleedin' hell, what's all this spew
                floating in the air? And what's Willy doing on the
                ceiling?

Frank: (Desperately trying to save the show) Er... nothing
                Arthur. We've got a... er... thingy... you know...
                one of... Bleuuurrrggghhhhh... those... er poltergeist
                wotsits. That's it. I forgot to mention it. The
                Queen Vic's haunted... by the ghost of Dirty Den,
                innit?

Dr Legge: That's nothing Arthur. My... Bleuuurrrggghhhhh...
                half of bitter is floating out of its glass in...
                Bleuuurrrggghhhhh... globules (Jumps in air, trying
                to catch globules in mouth)

Pat: You know they told us to keep our... Bleuuurrrggghhh
                ... hand over the top of the glass at all...
                Bleuuurrrggghhhhh... times.

Frank: Ah... yes, Doctor, er... it's a new beer we're trying
                out. It's extra light... Bleuuurrrggghhhhh...

Ethel: What's he talking about? I don't remember anything
                like this in the script.

Sharon: Bleuuurrrggghhhhh...

Arthur: Now look what your Willy's done!

Ethel: Bleuuurrrggghhhhh... All this floating about has
                made him excited.

Dr Legge: Now there's... Bleuuurrrggghhhhh... globules of dog's
                urine mixing with my beer. How do I... Bleuuurrggghhhh
                ... know which is which?

Ali:	(Rushing on to the set, covered in blood) I've just seen Colin's helmet!
Everyone:	Bleuuurrrggghhhhh...
Ali:	He was in the air lock. There must have been a pressure leak, because it swelled up to four times its normal size!
Everyone:	Bleuuurrrggghhhhh...
Ali:	Before exploding!
Everyone:	Bleuuurrrggghhhhh... bbbbllllluuuuuuurrrrgh!

(Hurried rolling of credits)

The Great Predicto also believes that BBC Radio will follow television into space, and programmes like this will become fairly commonplace...

Simon Bates:	That was the new one from Kylie Minogue! And yes, it really does sound like that and it's not because of zero gravity up here! My special guest today is - wait for it, girls - Matt from Bros! Good morning Matt!
Matt:	'Kinell! Does weightlessness always feel like this?
Simon Bates:	Ha ha! First time in space eh, Matt?
Matt:	Oh... shit, I... I... I... BLURRRRRRRPPP!
Simon Bates:	Oh... well, I'll be talking to Matt in just a few minutes. First, here on Radio 1, some more spaced-out sounds with...
(LOUD CRASH)	
(Voice off-mike):	Shit! Shit! Shit! I put my hand in it!
Simon Bates:	Er... ha, ha! Guess what, gang? Abby, everyone's favourite space cadet, just floated in and dropped the coffee capsules.. Ha, ha, ha! While she goes down to the cargo bay to find some more, let's hear the title track from the new Bros album...
Matt:	BLUUUURRRRRRPP! OHHHHHHH! BLU-BLU-BLUUURRRRRRRRRRRRPPP! Oh. God... ohhhh...
Simon Bates:	Well, I'm sure we've got another copy of the album around here someplace...
Matt:	Look out... it's spreading all over the turntable...

Simon Bates:	While we try and track down another copy, I'll carry on talking to my special guest, Matt from Bros...
Matt:	BLURRRRP!
Simon Bates:	Oh shit! Oh Christ! Not again!
Matt:	Sorry, mate. Is that a new jacket?
Simon Bates:	That's OK! Alexander O'Neil threw up on it last week... Now, on the new album, you and your brother Luke have written most of the songs and, a little bird tells...
Matt:	Better take it off, mate. It's floatin' over the back of your neck... Oh God, I wanna lie down...
Simon Bates:	Er, ha ha! You in fact wrote the title track, which...
Matt:	I'm serious, mate, I've gotta lie down somewhere... ohhhhhhh... Jesus...
Simon Bates:	Hey Matt! Watch out for that hovering spew cloud! Um. Er...
Matt:	Oh Jesus, it's all over the place... BLURRRRP! BLURRRRP!
Simon Bates:	Thanks, Matt, it's been great having you on board. Tomorrow, I'll be talking to Five Star.
Matt:	URRRRPPPPP!

WILL ROMANCE BE A THING OF THE PAST?

Unquiet spirits from the other side regularly visit at Barbara Burke at home – much to the horror of her husband Dennis, who has stayed barricaded in the bedroom for the past five years.

'Recently a bloody, skull-faced apparition in a red cloak dropped by,' she told us, in an interview conducted from about as far away in the UK as we could get. He said that in the early 1990s major professions such as insurance, advertising, banking and estate agencies will be full of wankers.'

BARBARA BURKE

Well, little or no change there, you might say... But Mrs Burke's dread apparition was speaking *literally*.
'He said that these people are too busy to have romances and too scared of AIDS to have sex with anyone.'
And the 'dirty weekend' in Brighton could be a very different thing in future...

Hotel Brighton
REGISTRATION BOOK

DATE	NAME	ADDRESS	ROOM No.	TYPE
3/2/91	mr. J Smith	4 The Road	4	Single
3/2/91	Mr J Smith	10 Downing St.	6	Single
3·2·91	Mr P Daniels	c/o The BBC	7	Single

'Singles magazines, rather than trying to bring people together, will be showing them how to live happily by themselves...'

Price **£2.00**

February 1991

Singles

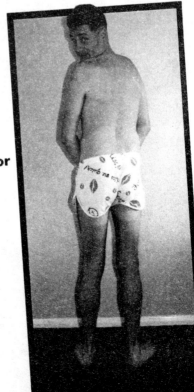

* **Breaking up — could YOU cope with schizophrenia!**

* **The problem with 'surprise gifts' — a few practical solutions**

* **We test drive the new 'Stud-O-Matic Wangmaster 2000' vibrator**

* **Craving variety? Have you considered a sex change?**

* **How to be the person you always wanted to come home to!**

* **Some guys have all the luck! What it's like to be double jointed...**

* **Orgasm — how to tell if you're faking it!**

'Valentines' Day, too, will be radically altered, not least because you'll always know who sent the card...'

To 'A'. The man I see in the bathroom mirror every morning at 7.15.
Lots of hugs, Ashley.

Lisa. You're always there when I need you. Be mine forever, Lisa.

Eric. Only you know my true feelings. Kissie, Kissie, love 'E'

Cat. I missed you when I was in my coma. Thanks for waiting. Cat XXX

Kermit be forever mine, Kermit.

J.C. Sorry if I neglect you sometimes. Thanks for being so understanding. Your loving J.C.

J.C. I know your career must come first, but I'll wait for you. J.C.

Chubby Chops luvs Chubby Chops XXXX

Gareth. Since the day we were born, I've known you were the only one for me. Always yours. G

Peterkins. Love, hugs, fondles and kisses, sexy britches! Love Peterkins XXX

David. Hope you like the card. I thought of you when I saw it! Love David XXX

'And, most significantly of all, we'll see an end to all those compilation albums full of old love songs. Instead, they'll release compilation albums based on... um... self love...'

Twenty Magnificent Chart-Topping Songs for Loving Singles!

SIDE 1

Bachelor Boy — Cliff Richard
Beat It — Michael Jackson
Big Spender — Shirley Bassey
Did You Ever — Nancy Sinatra
First Thing in the Morning — Kiki Dee
(Get a) Grip (on Yourself) — The Stranglers
God's Gonna Punish You — The Thymes
Good Vibrations — The Beach Boys
Hard Habit to Break — Chicago
I Knocked it Off — B A Robertson

SIDE 2

My Favourite Waste of Time — Owen Paul
My Way — Frank Sinatra
Pump it Up — Elvis Costello and the Attractions

Rock-a-Beatin' Boogie — Bill Haley and the Comets
See Emily Play — Pink Floyd
Sisters Are Doin' it for Themselves — Eurythmics and Aretha Franklin

Soul Finger — The Bar-Kays
We All Follow Manchester United — Manchester United Football Team
We Do It — R and J Stone
Whatever Gets You Through the Night — John Lennon

WILL KYLIE MINOGUE'S GREATEST HITS DESTROY THE WORLD?

 Many psychics claim they can see the future in tea leaves. Julia Ross does things a *little* differently – she uses pizza toppings. 'I order a pizza with everything, ' she explains. 'It's all to do with the arrangement of the little bits and pieces. I mean, theoretically, you could do the same with a puddle of puke, but this way's a lot more pleasant.' We agree, and take her to the local Pizza Hut to put her claims to the test. When Julia's pizza finally arrives, her face turns deathly white. 'It's worse than I thought... a black olive in the third quarter touching an anchovy! We're looking at a disaster of global proportions! They're going to set up this huge computer called SHOP-1, which will buy and sell things all over the world,' she explains. 'And everyone will order all their shopping electronically through their television sets. It will be free to automatically buy whatever it wants, negotiate the price and then resell at a

JULIA ROSS

profit on behalf of its owners, an American company called Homeshop Inc. It will have to operate by established laws of trading, though. For example, it will only be able to sell goods of merchantable quality and fit for the purpose for which made.' We stare at Julia's pizza. It looks like an ordinary pizza. She pours herself another glass of wine. 'And that's where the trouble will start…'

Thanks to the Pizza Hut 9" deep pan with extra toppings, we have a psychic timetable of disaster…

17 NOV 1995   The first hint of trouble. SHOP-1 is offered 500,000 copies of the expected Christmas smash *Kylie Minogue's Greatest Hits* but consistently refuses to offer them for sale. Eventually its programme is overridden.

DEC 1995   Christmas chaos as thousands of customers receive the wrong presents from the supposedly infallible SHOP-1.

1 JAN 1996   It is noticed that something has gone badly wrong with SHOP-1, after Mrs Conelly of Belmont Circle orders a pair of slacks for her husband–and receives the *USS Nimitz* instead.

3 JAN 1996   Mrs Virash Shah of Madras, India, starts to receive Lake Huron through her letter box. *'All day long these tankers would come and pump water and fish and underwater plant life into our house. Well, they had all the right paperwork, so I presumed it was something my husband had ordered'* she says.

4 JAN 1996   The Roman Catholic Church is rocked by the revelation that Pope John Paul has apparently ordered twenty-five 'Stretchy Lovemaster' Penis Enlargers, which turn up at the Vatican with huge labels saying 'PENIS ENLARGERS FOR THE POPE'. After a period of quiet, John Paul makes a less-than-satisfactory denial saying that, if anything, he requires a penis reducer and is not seen in public again.

5 JAN 1996   Over a period of twenty-four hours, actress and singer Kylie Minogue receives 800 lb of dung, several sharks, 900,000 gallons of liquid nitrogen, a puma, an unspecified quantity of Strontium 90, 456 bottles of strychnine labelled 'Diet Cola', four pythons, two black mambas, 345 kilos of Semtex plastic explosive marked 'Yum Yum Soft Toffee', thirty-two merchant seamen who haven't seen a woman since October and a rabid beaver.

Luckily, she is away recording a new album.

31 JAN 1996   Millions of people receive their Homeshop statements and discover they are completely bankrupt. Included are fully legal possession orders for their homes and worldly goods. Banks collapse as customers' life savings are transferred to Homeshop in settlement.

4 FEB 1996   Homeshop promise to repay all moneys seized by SHOP-1, only to discover that SHOP-1 has already ploughed all the money back into purchasing new products for sale.

6 FEB 1996   Kylie Minogue returns to what remains of her home and recovers her Homeshop statement. It simply says 'KYLIE MUST DIE'… over one million times.

16 APR 1996   Kylie Minogue realises that there might just be something significant about her statement and hands it in to her nearest Homeshop office.

With utter horror, computer experts realise what has happened to SHOP-1. It has been programmed to buy and sell goods 'only of a merchantable quality', as per international law, but has, at the same time, been instructed to sell *Kylie Minogue's Greatest Hits*… and the resulting conflict in its logic circuits has driven it incurably insane and malevolent.

1 MAY 1996   Attempts by SHOP-1's owners, Homeshop Inc., to shut down the computer are foiled when SHOP-1 offers itself on the market and rapidly purchases itself with the aid of an off-the-shelf company it buys in London. It is now private property and cannot be touched.

5 MAY 1996   Attempts to stop SHOP-1 by taking it to court for serious trading malpractices are foiled when it buys the Freemasons and the case is instantly dismissed.

10 MAY 1996   SHOP-1 buys the entire western gold reserves and then offers the gold to customers at £1.70 per metric tonne (inc. postage and packing). Mrs Y Levaine of Grenoble is first on the button and purchases it all. She refuses to give it back and becomes the most powerful

Disaster! Mrs Conelly orders trousers but instead finds herself proud owner of the aircraft carrier the USS Nimitz.

person in the world. The stockmarket crashes and there are four-hour tailbacks on window ledges in London, New York and Tokyo.

11 MAY 1996 Russian Premiere Gorbachev receives a scrubbing brush and eight tonnes of scouring powder from SHOP-1, together with a note saying *'Dear Pissface, try using this to get rid of that horrible pukey birthmark. It makes me want to toss my cookies every time I sit across the summit table from you.'* It is apparently signed by the President of the United States. Gorbachev immediately retaliates by sending the President half the world's existing supplies of deodorant and two sticks of dynamite *'To get the skidmarks out of your jockey shorts.'* The world trembles on the brink of war…

12 MAY 1996 SHOP-1 sells two-thirds of America's nuclear stockpile to Colonel Gaddafi for 49p. Luckily, they are misrouted in transit and end up on the doorstep of Mrs G Rodgers of Weston-super-Mare, where they are eventually safely defused. *'We all had a good laugh about it later,'* says Mrs Rodgers, *'although I shat my drawers at the time!'*

16 MAY 1996 SHOP-1 demands that Kylie Minogue must be sacrificed to it, or it will continue to plunge the world into chaos.

30 MAY 1996 Computer experts hit upon a desperate plan to save the world. If SHOP-1 has been driven insane by the contradictions of selling *Kylie Minogue's Greatest Hits,* how will it react to even worse produce?

2 JUNE 1996 Every factory in the world has been converted to selling only faulty and useless products. The following weeks see the introduction of thousands of new substandard or offensive products, including Highland Smegma Whiskey, *Bonnie Langford: The Video, Learn To Sing the Rolf Harris Way,* sholleys covered in pictures of dead babies, pre-stained underwear, baths with taps at *both* ends, sweat shirts with twelve sleeves saying 'I Love Rubella', tinned vomit in brine, videos that will only record the weather forecast, copies of *The Wind in the Willows* translated into Carthaginian, Mother's Day cards saying 'Piss off and die, fat thighs!', a new line of tampons – for men, Bernard Manning's *Guide to Gracious Living*… and *Kylie Minogue's Greatest Hits, Volume Two*…

12 JUNE 1996 SHOP-1 realises that it has been outsmarted and commits commercial suicide by putting itself up for sale at just 2p. Mrs Dot Bannister of Warminster snaps it up, resells it to the United Nations for £7 million and goes off to live in the Virgin Islands.

13 JUNE 1996 The United Nations dismantle SHOP-1.

9 DEC 1996 Work begins on the assembly of the new, 'infallible' SHOP-2.

10 DEC 1996 Jason Donovan has his ninth consecutive solo hit…

WHAT FUTURE IS THERE FOR BRITAIN'S NATIONAL HEALTH SERVICE?

None.

But it doesn't take a psychic to tell you that. So we didn't spend much time with Mrs Yvette Mason, who resides in Eastbourne.

Before we set off to the beach for a pose (and a quick paddle), Mrs Mason told us that the National Health Service will be made fully autonomous and allowed to charge what it wants and to promote its services however it wishes, in an attempt to turn hospitals into effective, streamlined business operations...

What does that mean?
Basically, it means this...

EASTBOURNE

ST SWITHINS HOSPITAL
OPERATIONS
OPTIONAL EXTRAS PRICE LIST

(This price list is correct as of going to press on 3 August 1993, but may be subject to quite alarming price jumps without prior warning.)

Anaesthetic *(local)*	£ 70.00
Anaesthetic *(general)*	140.00

(Please note we recommend the purchase of a general anaesthetic for serious and prolonged operations.)

Taxi trolley to the operating theatre *(Includes price of admission. Gratuities at discretion of patient)*	12.00
Admission to operating theatre	4.50
Clean surgical instruments	226.00

Choice of surgeon's medical grade:
– Guaranteed senior surgeon	4,400.00
– Guaranteed qualified junior surgeon	1,700.00
– Low-cost first year medical student option	175.00
– Some loony who's wandered into the hospital wearing a white coat and pretending he's a surgeon	249.00
Hire of heart-monitoring instrumentation	378.00
Nurses to assist surgeon (price is per nurse)	150.00
Stitches to close incision (catgut)	7.50
Stitches to close incision (nylon)	6.50
Stitches to close incision (silk)	8.99
Staples to close incision	4.99
Scotch tape to close incision	3.99
(Please note price is per stitch)	
Taxi trolley service back to ward	7.99

The above prices are exclusive of VAT. A 25% surcharge will be added to all purchase prices. Patients with a St Swithin's Patient Plus charge card are entitled to a 5% discount.

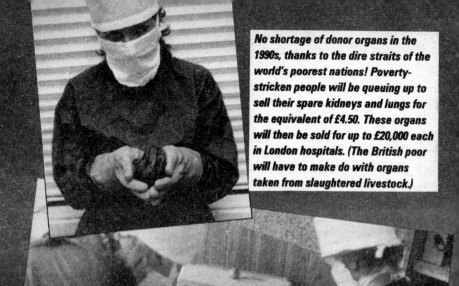

No shortage of donor organs in the 1990s, thanks to the dire straits of the world's poorest nations! Poverty-stricken people will be queuing up to sell their spare kidneys and lungs for the equivalent of £4.50. These organs will then be sold for up to £20,000 each in London hospitals. (The British poor will have to make do with organs taken from slaughtered livestock.)

Anxious surgeons continuously monitor their patient's credit rating during a complicated heart by-pass operation.

DONOR KIDNEY CHARGE RATES –

ST MALCOLMS

May 1993

£

1. Kidney of Western origin	37,000.00
2. Kidney of Third World origin	20,000.00
3. Kidney of unspecified primate	8,800.00
4. Kidney of other animal	5,500.00
5. Kidney of Turk	40.00

Please note that these charges are intended only as a guide and may depend on the exchange rate of the pound against the Ethiopian Birr, the Nigerian Naira and the Gabonese CFA Franc at the time of purchase.

We are also licenced credit brokers. Ask about our generous low-interest HP plans and special 'Organ Back' deals on your death.

Would You Like to be Free of Your
Dialysis Machine...

... BUT CAN'T AFFORD A TRANSPLANT?

- Ask about our exciting new 'Organ Timeshare' deals!
- A kidney of your own... for three weeks a year, every year!
- Call St George's Hospital now on Freephone Organ!

St Bernards

NOW WART REMOVAL NEEDN'T COST YOU AN ARM AND A LEG!
JUST A KIDNEY!

If you're unhappy about that ugly, grotesque, unsightly, disfiguring wart that's probably spoiling your chances of finding a boyfriend (and ever getting married and having children), come to St Bernard's!

We'll whip it off and subject it to a free biopsy as well! (It could be cancerous, but you'll never know if you don't have it removed.)

And best of all it won't cost you a penny! No, just one of your kidneys is all we charge for this operation. You've got two, and you probably won't even know it's gone!

Bring that horrible lump of gnarled, potentially cancerous disease to our dermatology department today – and say goodbye to all your boyfriend problems!

Those Crazy Medics at St Kilda's Are at it Again!

ORGAN BONANZA!

LOWEST PRICES GUARANTEED ON HEARTS, LUNGS, KIDNEYS AND LIVERS!

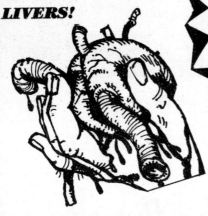

THERE'S NEVER BEEN A BETTER TIME TO HAVE AN ORGAN TRANSPLANT!

Thanks to a spate of recent disasters at home and in Europe, we've got literally thousands of good quality vital organs that we're selling at crazy, givaway prices!

Hearts from just £40,000!

Lungs from just £20,000!

Kidneys from just £15,950!

Livers from just £19,999!

All guaranteed only one owner. No reconditioned or damaged organs, either! Come and inspect them for yourself, before you buy! If you've got a strong stomach that is (and if you haven't, we can do you a new one of those as well from just £9,999 plus VAT!).

And remember, you get your money back if your body rejects the organ!

▷▷▷ **IF YOU DON'T BUY AT THESE PRICES YOU NEED A BRAIN TRANSPLANT!**

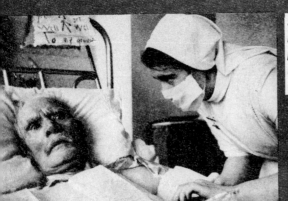

Sister Cindy Ryan of the Great Metropolitan Hospital in Leeds tells a patient his condition is terminal – and makes him a generous offer for his eyes and vital organs.

A visiting relative stops passers–by in a desperate attempt to get some more ten pences for her loved one's life support machine. Coin-operated oxygen tents and drip feeds will also be a common sight in the 1990s and many heart-attack patients will die because they haven't got change for the resuscitation machine.

YOU TAKE CARE OF YOUR ORGANS – AND WE'LL TAKE CARE OF YOU!

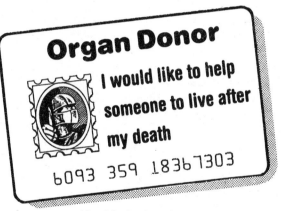

Organ Donor

I would like to help someone to live after my death

6093 359 18367303

Pass our scrupulous personal health check and YOU could qualify for a St Dominic's Gold Organ Donor Card.

● It's a donor card *and* a credit card accepted at over two million establishments worldwide, all in one!

● Plus, it entitles you to valuable discounts off fast cars and motorbikes, skydiving weekends, white water rapid canoeing, and holidays in Belfast and Londonderry.

● But the benefits don't stop there.

● In the unfortunate event of you being involved in a fatal accident, we'll take more care in removing your donor organs.

● Like, we'll make sure you're actually dead first.

St Dominic's Gold Organ Donor Card.
Don't do anything dangerous without it.

Toy manufacturers, sensitive to criticisms that they are producing toys which glorify war and mindless violence to children, will be offering produce new types of toys in the 1990s - ones with a refreshingly religious slant...

WATCH OUT! SAY YOUR PRAYERS, EVIL-DOERS...

TRANSFORM-ICONS™

ARE HERE!

Icons of the Blessed Virgin Mary and Saints that transform in seconds into death-dealing robots, ready and waiting to do battle with the dreaded Satanoids™!

MARY™ – calm and serene in any crisis, she's the leader of the heroic Transform-Icons™ and mother of Jesus Christ our Saviour. Turns into a formidable battle robot with **laser fists** and an **ecclesiastical photon buzzsaw!**

ST STEPHEN™ - Mary's™ right-hand man. Hot-tempered, but with nerves of titanium steel! Annihilates Satanoids™ with his **MX Nuclear Missile Arms and Cyclops Laser Death Glare!**

ST IGNATIOUS, the Blessed Martyr™ – sacrifices himself to save the Transform-Icons™ from certain destruction by flying into the heart of Satanoid™ death hordes – and then blowing himself up!

ST FRANCIS™ – the weapons specialist and patron saint of animals. Transforms into **Battlehawk**™, swooping down to deal death and destruction to the Satanoids™ with his **New Testament Terror Talons!**

ST JEROME™ – most feared of all the Transform-Icons™. Changes from mild-mannered patron saint into a beserker robot with **glowing cyborg eyes** and a **chest pulsar cannon** capable of obliterating whole galaxies!

FIGHT THE GOOD FIGHT AGAINST THE DREADED SATANOIDS™

Born Again Bunny

He's heard the word of the Lord – and now YOU can hear the words of Born Again Bunny™*! The world's first Christian cuddly toy that really witnesses!*

Hallelujah!

Thank you some more, Jesus!

I've seen the light!

I was a sinner, but now I'm whole!

Thank you, Jesus!

I am saved!

Thank you, sweet Lord, for coming into my life!

THE FIRST SKODA
ON MARS!

 Nigel Rowbotham claims to be in telepathic communication with Martians, who have warned him that the joint US/USSR manned mission to Mars planned for the 1990s is destined to end in disaster.

It seems that in order to transmit effectively, the Martians needed someone whose limited intelligence facilitated the taking-over of his mind for short periods.

As an employee of Woolworths Nigel was perfect for their purposes and tried, repeatedly, to pass on their warnings to NASA, who in the end had to change their phone number.

Repeated warnings to the Russian Space Agency resulted in two men in black raincoats coming round to his store and kicking him in the bollocks; an act which he took as a subtle hint to stay out of the way.

In desperation Nigel has asked us to pass on the message received from his contacts. Being Martians and possessing natural psychic abilities, they have told him all aspects of the mission, past *and* future...

**NIGEL
ROWBOTHAM**

SECRET KEY DATES LEADING UP TO THE MISSION.

7 January 1988:
Mr Gorbachev calls President Reagan with his idea of a joint Soviet/American mission to Mars.

3 February 1988:
President Reagan has an emergency meeting with joint chiefs of staff in order to find out where Mars is. They order the CIA to launch a covert operation to locate the planet.

8 July 1988:
The CIA cannot pinpoint it more accurately than 'between Venus and Neptune'. They consider the whole exercise a Communist plot after it is discovered that Mars is known as the 'red planet'.

7 September 1988:
A chance remark to Nancy Reagan's astrologer solves the mystery of Mars' location. (President Reagan is also advised that it is a good day for making new friends.)

8 September 1988:
President Reagan contacts Mr Gorbachev, apologises for the eight-month delay and confirms his agreement in principle.

18 December 1988:
As one of his last decisions as president, Mr Reagan agrees the launch timetable. In 1994, two space craft will rendezvous in earth orbit. The US astronauts will then transfer to the Russian craft to begin their five-month journey to Mars.

12 January 1989:
It is announced that the American spacecraft will be built by a consortium (but absolutely nothing will be touched by Boeing).

TASS announces that the Russian craft has been subcontracted to Skoda in order to fill capacity in their production line (demand for the Estelle 1300LSE has been slack).

4 September 1990:
Mission in jeopardy when both countries fail to agree on a name for the Mars Landing Module.

6 January 1991:
After lengthy debates the UN General Assembly decides to name it after the only creature common to both countries – the Cockroach. Work on both spacecraft resumes.

7 July 1992:
In his first real job as president, Bush officially expresses concern over the technology inherent in the Russian spacecraft. He cites the 'deep freeze' chambers for the crew made from modified domestic refrigerators and rocket fuel which is a combination of liquid oxygen and vodka.

8 July 1992:
Mr Gorbachev tactfully informs President Bush to mind his own 'Damn Yankee business' and asks who lost seven astronauts in a shuttle disaster.

10 July 1992:
President Bush retaliates by calling Yuri

Gagarin a 'Goddamn nancy boy'. Mission in jeopardy once more as diplomatic relations are broken between the two powers.

26 July 1992:
Further meetings of the UN General Assembly result in a peace plan being agreed, including ratification that Yuri Gagarin was a 'Red-blooded Soviet hero with no record or reputation whatsoever of being involved in posterior liaisons with other men'.

Construction of both craft continues.

3 September 1993:
Both craft roll out for inspection and engines undergo test firing. Soviet craft suffers setback when it is discovered that the fuel pump and starter motor need replacing under warranty.

7 March 1994:
All systems go! The rockets are launched.

THE MISSION

1 US spacecraft lifts off from Cape Kennedy on time.

2a The Soviet spacecraft fails to lift off, due to the excess weight of seventeen KGB agents hidden on board.

2b Soviet craft successfully relaunched. Flight path erratic due to cosmonauts drinking rocket fuel immediately prior to take off.

3 Docking successfully carried out. However, it takes American astronauts over nine hours to enter the Russian craft because they cannot understand the Cyrillic for 'PUSH BAR TO OPEN'.

4 Russian craft with US astronauts on board begins trajectory for Mars.

5 One cosmonaut defects during unauthorised space walk.

6 Both crews are frozen for the five-month journey. (One astronaut develops salmonella poisoning after he is accidentally defrosted too early and then re-frozen.)

7 Russian craft misses Mars orbital rendezvous as cosmonauts have neglected to wind up their onboard Sekonda watch.
   Ship has to turn round and achieves successful orbit on the second attempt.

8 Mars Landing Module begins descent.

9 15.32 GMT, 8 September 1994: 'The Cockroach has landed'.

10 Scuffle in airlock of landing module as both crews try to be first on the surface.

11 Exploration work carried out; officially, no trace of Martian life is reported. In reality, contact is made almost immediately with representatives of the Martian race, but since by a strange quirk of nature the Martians all resemble Richard Gere naked, none of the crew admit to seeing one.

12 Crews prepare to leave planet, only to find that someone forgot to turn landing module lights off. The flat battery makes it impossible to lift off. Both crews slowly die through lack of oxygen.

THE HISTORIC FIRST TRANSMISSION FROM MARS

[Crackle – crackle]

LT. COLLINS: OK men, prepare to leave the airlock.

MAJOR SUKAROV: Let me through, impudent American pig boy!

LT. COLLINS: Now just a minute, Major! It was agreed that I'd be the first out on to Mars.

MAJOR SUKAROV: That was eight months ago. I've received coded instructions during the flight which countermand your orders. Now move out of my way, imperialist scum.

(Sounds of a scuffle and air escaping)

CAPT. BROOKES: It's OK Lieutenant. I've got him… oooff!

MAJOR IVANOVICH: No you haven't, Yankee demon. Major, make a run for it!

(More scuffles)

LT. GORDON: We were prepared for this. Right men. 41.28.34. Hike!

(More scuffles)

MAJOR TOSCOV: Watch out for Gordon! He's playing wide and flanked our defences…

LT. GORDON: Touch down! Right. I name that crater over there 'John Wayne Crater'.

MAJOR SUKAROV: *(Scrambling down ladder)* Nyet. It is 'Leon Trotsky Craterski'. And that is 'Blood of the Founding Bolsheviks Rille'.

LT. GORDON: Horseshit it is! That's 'Joe Dimaggio Ridge'.

CAPT. BROOKES: *(Scrambling down ladder)* Hey you guys! Look over there! Do you see what I see? Shit! It looks like 240 naked Richard Geres!

MISSION CONTROL: Say again please Cockroach. Over.

CAPT. BROOKES: Oh. Did I say '240 naked Richard Geres'? I meant lots of… red rocks and things… and dust… and bits. Over.

MARTIAN VOICE: Greetings Earthmen, from the bottom of our podules. We welcome you to Mars.

MISSION CONTROL: Who the fuck was that, Cockroach? Over.

LT. GORDON: Oh… No one. No one at all…

CAPT. BROOKES: … Er… I was just saying out loud what I would say, if I were a Martian… um… which, of course, I couldn't be because there aren't any. Especially any that look like Richard Gere, naked. Over.

MARTIAN VOICE:	Hey, Earthmen, you've left your landing lights on.
LT. GORDON:	Did any of you men hear anything then?
CAPT. BROOKES:	Couldn't have done, could I?
MAJOR SUKAROV:	Nyet.
LT. COLLINS:	I don't know what you're talking about.
MAJOR IVANOVICH:	Nyet. I'm perfectly sane.
MAJOR TOSCOV:	Me too. I have the Peoples Commendation for Saneness.
MARTIAN VOICE:	Suit yourselves. Don't say we didn't warn you.

THE FIRST SKODA ON MARS

Unlike the Americans, the Soviet philosophy in developing hardware for their space programme is to make the best use of existing technology. The Russian 'Mars Roving Vehicle' (MRV) is based on the tried and tested Skoda 130GL whose standard features such as comprehensive tool kit (inc. spare bulbs and fuses), locking glove box (suitable for keeping samples of Mars' rock) and heated rear window (useful when traversing Mars' polar ice caps) make it an ideal choice.

Of course, operating on the inhospitable surface of Mars, with its total lack of oxygen and temperatures ranging from −135°C to +280°C means that certain modifications are needed for it to function properly as a mobile communications and exploration centre.

The most important of these are the fixing of large, 'balloon' tyres for increased traction on Mars' sandy terrain, and replacement of the standard elastic band with a high-tensile tungsten steel belt.

WHY WILL THE POLICE BRING A BOTTLE WHEN THEY RAID PARTIES?

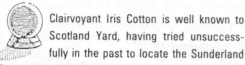

Clairvoyant Iris Cotton is well known to Scotland Yard, having tried unsuccessfully in the past to locate the Sunderland Slayer, the Bognor Regis Pubic Fiend and the Lincolnshire Plumber by her psychic powers – even though the police had never heard of these felons, and weren't looking for them.

Her most recent vision showed her what Britain's police force would be like in the 1990s – if they followed the recommendations of a 1991 Home Office study into public attitudes towards the police.

According to Iris, the report will conclude that, in order to win respect from the young, the police must change their whole image in an effort to make themselves 'less authoritarian' and more like a 'bloody good mate'...

IRIS COTTON

1. POLICE STATIONS

In order to make these more user-friendly it is recommended that their premises be redesigned to resemble locations where the young will feel more at home, i.e. wine bars. Each police station in a town will therefore be refurbished.

In these new premises, the front desk should resemble a bar complete with video CD jukebox, and condom/hyperdermic syringe dispensing machines should be located in the toilets.

The term 'police station' sounds uninviting and perhaps even threatening. To avoid sounding menacing and anonymous, each police station should have its own unique identity.

Other COP SHOPS in this area:
BLUEBOTTLES, South Harrow
HELMETS, Edgware
THE TRUNCHEON CLUB, Kenton
TROTTER'S, Burnt Oak

2. TRANSPORT

A) POLICE PATROL VEHICLES:

The Rover and Granada cars currently in use are felt to be too authoritarian. A car appealing to, and respected by, the young male is therefore preferable.

Tape loop playing I fought the law (and the law won) by The Clash to replace the conventional siren
▷

Driver and co-driver will be easily identified
▷

Disco lights to replace the traditional blue lamp
◁

△
Officers may customise their patrol cars as they see fit

B) BICYCLES:

The current police bicycle has its roots in the 1930s and is the subject of universal ridicule by the young. It is therefore recommended that ten-speed mountain bikes are adopted, with roller skates or skateboards being used by the more athletic constables.

3. UNIFORM AND ACCESSORIES

The current blue serge uniform should be adapted so that it is sympathetic to contemporary fashion trends, yet still retaining an air of authority.

▷
Diamante brooches will denote rank

▷
Jackets retained (but worn with sleeves rolled up between wrist and elbow, as featured in Miami Vice*)*

▷
Cool sunglasses to be worn all year round

▷
Shirt and tie replaced by white t-shirt with the word 'COP' in bold black letters

▷
Handcuffs and truncheons replaced by a new range of 'designer restrainers' in a variety of pastel colours designed to enhance the fashion look of the detainee

▷
Copofax (this is a police personal organiser)

▷
Boots replaced by Adidas, Nike or Reebok trainers

Walkie-talkies replaced by eighty watts per channel ghetto blasters to assist credibility in ethnically sensitive areas
▽

△
Trousers fashionably baggy

4. POLICE BEHAVIOUR

Despite their new image, the police will be expected to enforce the law with the same high standards, although discretion will be given to individual officers in the way that they choose to present a friendlier face to the public.

For example, they might only feel it polite to bring a bottle or six-pack with them when called to investigate noise complaints about a late-night party. Above all, an officer should strive to appear as 'a good bloke', rather than a symbol of authority and repression...

AMERICA'S FIRST CHIMPANZEE VICE PRESIDENT!

 Mrs Maggie Blundell accidentally fell out of a window on the 128th floor of the Empire State Building on to her head. She miraculously survived and ever since then she claims to be in telepathic communication with Michael Jackson's pet chimpanzee, Bubbles.

'Bubbles has the very rare gift of being a psychic monkey. All I do is pick up his simian thoughtwaves and pass them on to anyone who's interested, if I can find them…'

Mrs Blundell claims that Michael Jackson has long wanted to run for president but it will not be until 1996 that he is white enough to stand any chance of winning.

BUBBLES

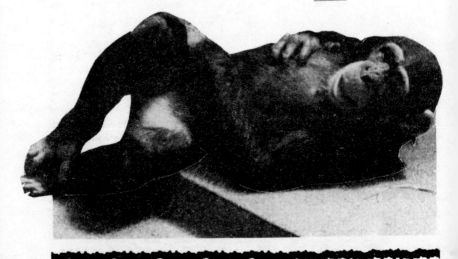

★★★★★★★★★★★★★★★★★★★★★★★★★

'Through Bubbles, I foresaw Michael announce himself as an independent candidate, knowing he would appeal to most sectors of society, young, white, black, male, female and asexual, since he seems to belong to all these categories.

'Then I saw Michael announce that Bubbles would be his running mate, since as a chimp, his past isn't cloaked in scandal (apart from the Los Angeles banana incident with the showgirl, but that was a complete accident).

'During 1995 I could see Michael Jackson on the campaign trail, playing free concerts in every city. Through Bubbles' ears I heard his campaign song *White House,* played non-stop from coast to coast. Do you want to hear it?'

Despite our protests, Mrs Blundell sang us the campaign song, accompanying herself on the Bontempi.

W H I T E H O U S E

By Michael Jackson © 1995

(sung to the tune of *Thriller*)

Verse 1:
It's close to voting
I want to get the job of president
I'll be a nice one
You'll have to take my word that I'm not bent
So vote me in
I will declare the world a place of fun
And if I win
I'll turn it into one big Disneyland
That's what I've planned.

Chorus:
'Cause this is White House, White House time
And I am gonna be there
If they don't lock me away
You know it's White House, White House time
You're gonna vote me into
The Big House, the White House, right now.

Verse 2:
Now my pet monkey
Will also be an honest candidate
His name is Bubbles
And I'll get him to be my running mate
Since he's a chimp
There won't be dirt or any type of scandal
But he's no wimp
To Playmates of the month, he'll just say 'Nix!'
He'll say, 'No monkey tricks!'

[Repeat Chorus]

Rap:
(Performed by Vincent Price)
Voting starts across the land
The final count is close at hand
Michael's strange – his brain has gone
He'll be just like good old Ron
Presidential nutters came and went
But how many slept in an oxygen tent?
Even though Michael's a sickie
He can't be worse than Tricky Dicky
The world is screwed enough already
But Michael's got his lucky teddy
And with his llama and his latex face
He'll make the States a better place
The time has come for all his fans
To help make him into a man
And though he squeaks just like a mouse
He'll end up here – in the White House.

(Demonic laughter that fades out...)

Maggie continued, 'Michael's policies, his campaign song and the fact that his vice president hasn't slept with his secretary, isn't an ex-alcoholic and hasn't evaded the draft, will lead to a landslide win. After the inauguration ceremony, Bubbles will be forced to spend two months in quarantine before being able to make foreign trips (being only the second vice president to undergo this period of confinement). President Jackson will then bring the US back to a period of prosperity last seen in the fifties.

'As a token of its appreciation the Senate will add Michael Jackson's face to those already carved into Mount Rushmore.'

Mrs Blundell had to leave at this point since it was time for her convulsion therapy. Her parting words as she was assisted to the ambulance were, 'Bubbles wants you to know that I'm not crazy! He has a personal message for you. He says, "Ooooooh! Ooooooh! Oooh-Oooh-Oooh! Screech! S c r e e c h ! O o h - O o h - O o h ! Screeeeeeechhhh! Oooooooooh! Ooh-Ooh-Oooooohhhhhhhhh!"'

We went to a leading zoologist for a translation. He told us to go fuck ourselves. Bubbles' last message to us remains a tantalising enigma…

Much to the annoyance of the National Parks Commission, Mount Rushmore will be permanently spoilt by scaffolding as President Jackson undergoes incessant cosmetic surgery and his monument has to be continually resculpted

WILL BRITAIN'S CITIES BE CONSUMED IN NUCLEAR FIRE?

Francesca Watkins has a very special friend — Chief Ironcloud, her faithful Indian spirit guide.

We ask her why spirit guides are always Red Indian Chiefs. She shrugs. (You often get answers like that when you delve into the occult.)

'Chief Ironcloud tells me many things... like if my slip is showing, or if I need to blow my nose, things like that. But sometimes he talks about the future. Often, I can't quite understand him, because he's a very clichéd Red Indian. Have you any idea what "Heap Big Wampum" is?'

We shake our heads (although we suspect it might be a derogatory term for Paul Daniels).

'Anyway, his last message to me was: "White man speak with forked tongue... and none more so than Palefaces working in the nuclear power industries! Ug! Heap bad medicine!

'"Before many moons, they will sellum tiny nuclear reactors to heap load of people to put in teepees..." '

FRANCESCA WATKINS AND CHIEF IRONCLOUD

THE BROWNS GET IT RIGHT!

THE MOST COMMONLY ASKED QUESTIONS ABOUT MINI NUCLEAR REACTORS

WILL THEY BLOW UP?
That's not one of the most commonly asked questions, so there's no need to cover that point here.

I'LL BET IT IS ONE OF THE MOST COMMONLY ASKED QUESTIONS.
Suprisingly, it isn't. Most people have faith in British technology. They know that, in this country, there are laws against selling shoddy, dangerous products.

LIKE EGGS ... AND THALIDOMIDE?
Look, you have our guarantee that our mini nuclear reactors are completely safe. Now, can we get back to the most commonly asked questions, like ...

I'M NO NUCLEAR ENGINEER. WHAT HAPPENS IF MY REACTOR NEEDS REPAIRS?
We offer a very cost-effective maintenance service and, in the event of reactor failure, we will dispatch an unmanned remote control drone repair vehicle from our base in the Orkneys within twenty-four hours!

WILL MY REACTOR COMPLETELY REPLACE GAS AND ELECTRICITY?
Of course! One mini reactor can produce enough power to run four hundred billion toasters simultaneously, and enough lights to illuminate the whole of Neptune, Uranus and Pluto. And, as the reactor is water-cooled by pumping the equivalent of Niagara Falls through it every seventeen seconds, it constantly produces enough steaming hot water to power over two million central heating systems.

Why, you can even sell surplus power to your neighbours, street or borough for handy spare cash!

ARE THERE ANY SIDE EFFECTS OF OWNING A MINI NUCLEAR REACTOR?
Yes! Your bank balance will be far healthier! Ha! Ha! Seriously, the answer is no, if you wear the suits provided and take your pills six times a day.

IF YOUR MINI REACTORS ARE SO SAFE, WHY ARE YOU BASED IN THE ORKNEYS?
We enjoy the rich and diverse wildlife on these far-flung isles.

WELL, THAT ANSWERS MY QUESTIONS! HOW DO I GET MY OWN MINI NUCLEAR REACTOR?
Simple! Just complete the form below and send it to us!

YES, I'm tired of paying extortionate electricity and gas bills! I want my very own mini nuclear reactor!
Please call me to arrange installation:

NAME:

ADDRESS:

POSTCODE   TEL. No. (DAY):

PLEASE COMPLETE AND RETURN TO:
STRONTIUM INDUSTRIES LTD, THE CAVERNS, NORTH RONALDSAY ISLAND, OUTERMOST ORKNEYS, SCOTLAND, ORK14 6WE.

Please note that, once you have purchased a mini nuclear reactor, you are liable for any and all consequences of its use. You are advised to extend your existing insurance policy to cover all dwellings in a forty kilometre radius and all farm animals between Eire and the Ukraine.

WILL JUDGEMENT DAY COME IN 1999?

'And in those last days shall come great signs in the skies!' cries pensioner Alfie Brookes, in the grip of religious rapture in his Peckham bedsit. His bloodshot eyes roll back in his skull and foam flecks his cracked and dried lips. 'Sort of like the illuminated ones you see in Piccadilly Circus, only of course they won't be advertising Coca Cola or Fuji film or anything like that! No! For they shall foretell that the Day of Judgement is at hand! And those who practise vice and cruelty and pervieness had better clean up their act pretty smartish!'

Alfie Brookes, it must be said has announced the end of the world eighteen times before. 'I was just practising then!' he tells us. 'But this time it's the real thing! Boys, you haven't been pervie-coveting thy neighbour's oxen recently, have you?'

We assure him we haven't.

'That's good. The Almighty hates that! It gets right up his nose!' Alfie bellows, his puny chest heaving.

ALFIE BROOKES

According to Alfie Brookes and his prophecies, here are a few of the warning signs we can expect to see in the skies in July 1999...

Repent!

HURRY!

World must end

31 August

1999!

There's Never Been a Better Time to Repent!

Hurry! Repent before 27 July and have all your previous sins forgiven without exception!*

*This offer does not apply to old Nazi war criminals, molesters of children and pervie-coveters of neighbour's oxen.

'Satan Wants Your Bottom!'

Yep, your ass is his if you don't do some serious repenting before 31 August! So, go to church today. And remember:

IT PAYS

TO PRAY!

Is Your Soul Radiant White with Purity and Mercy and Love?

Or is it stained with the skidmarks of lust, depravity, greed, sloth and the pervie-coveting of neighbour's oxen? Get it laundered at your church now!

'And on Earth, there shall be much consternation and going to the toilet. 'For a Heavenly Host of Angels shall start dismantling things. And the property speculators shall crieth out to the Lord, "For what do You disassemble our most wondrous works?" And the Lord shall replyeth, "Shut up, you greedy bastards! Thou didst abuseth My poorest children, for which sin thou shall wipe Demons' bottoms forever in the hottest corners of Gehenna's privvy!"'

We liked this bit a lot. Alfie pauses to take his medication, and then lets fly with more prophecy...

'And the US Marines shall confront the Angels of God and sayeth, "Hey, You ratfuck sons of bitches, stop dismantling the White House or we shall use our guns and tanks and helicopter gunships to blow Your asses back to Heaven!"'

Jesus shall return to Earth... several thousand miles off course.

According to Alfie Brookes, US Marines will confront the Angelic Host...

'And the Angels shall say unto the Army, "If thou couldst not defeat a bunch of short-arsed peasants in pyjamas, why dost think thou can destroy the assembled might of the armies of God? So, piss off!"

'And there shall come in that time the Antichrist, the Devil's bastard child, born of a drunken one-night stand with a beast of the field: he who will loose the Serpent of Twilight upon the Earth and make the radio to play only Conway Twitty and the willies of man to shrink so as to be derisory. And people will go, "Oh, no! It's the Antichrist!" and get out of his way pretty sharpish.

'And the Lord shall be affronted and say unto His only begotten son, "Go on Jesus, go and sort him out!"

'And Jesus shall descend to Earth in Madagascar for some unknown reason – while the Antichrist doth abide in Birmingham – and cry out "Eloi! Eloi! You work in some bloody mysterious ways sometimes!" and hitch a lift to the nearest airport.'

'And Jesus shall alight at Birmingham International Airport and the press shall be there and ask Him how He rates His chances of defeating the Antichrist and He shall sayeth unto them, "He's a good lad, Harry. He's strong and he's got a good right jab, but I'll take him inside four, dost thou know what I mean?"

'It shall come to pass that the National Exhibition Centre will be prepared for the fight of the millenium. And in those days, Harry Carpenter will be at the ringside to give his commentary...'

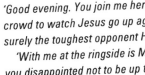

'Good evening. You join me here tonight with a capacity crowd to watch Jesus go up against the Antichrist... surely the toughest opponent He's ever had to face.

'With me at the ringside is Mohammed: Mohammed, are you disappointed not to be up there tonight? Pundits have been saying that many would prefer a Mohammed–Satan showdown...'

'Well, yes Harry, obviously I'm disappointed. I would have enjoyed fighting the ultimate evil, but our two camps could never agree on terms. I know Jesus: we've trained together on a number of occasions. He's not all He's made out to be, in my Book – but He deserves this chance.'

'Thank you, Mohammed. Right, both contestants are in the ring now, Jesus in the blue shorts, the Antichrist in the red. Jesus is looking good. He's obviously been training hard for this match. He's looking confident, enjoying a quick chat with John the Baptist in His corner... no doubt hoping to repeat the sort of form that had the moneylenders in the Temple in so much trouble.

'I've got to say that the Antichrist looks a bit edgy. He knows the money's against him and he's really got a fight on his hands here tonight.

'We're just seconds away from the bell now. Jesus's last outing ended in crucifixion of course, and there were those critics who thought He'd never come back from that one, but He told me in His dressing room earlier that, this time, He's back to stay and I for one believe Him.

'And that's the bell! The Antichrist has come out of his corner fast! He knows he's got to bring the fight to Jesus. And oh! He's kneed Jesus! He kneed Him! His satanic fury got the better of him and he just lashed out straight away! Jesus looks like He's in some pain... John the Baptist beside Him now in the ring... That was unforgivable! The Antichrist has got to be disqualified now...

'Yes, and it's all over! The Earth belongs to Jesus... and the Antichrist has been disqualified within just two seconds of round one! What a sensation!

'Well... that was the most shameful incident I've-ever seen in all my years in the ring... I'm going to try to fight my way through and have a few words with the winner...

'Jesus, can You tell the viewers at home how You feel?'

'Ohhhh! Myself! That hurt! I didn't even see it coming! I'm glad I won and everything, so that the souls of man may be redeemed, but... Ohhhhh!'

'I'm trying to have a word with John the Baptist now: John...'

'It's a disgrace! It's a bloody disgrace! We expected the Master of Evil to be a dirty fighter, but this is abso-bloody-lutely unforgivable! Barbaric! He's got to be kicked out of the game!'

'I'm with the Antichrist now! Antichrist, there have already been calls for you to be struck off and I must say, I agree with them...'

'Fuck off, Carpenter, you miserable human bag of mouldering slime and vomit! Or your mortal soul will be rent from your body and hurled screaming into the charnel depths of the pit!'

'Er... Over to you in the studio, David...'

Alfie starts convulsing as he talks, his limbs jerking and thrashing.

'And the Lord Jesus Christ shall establish unchallenged dominion over all the world and reign in majesty!' he cries. And He'll be much better at it than that bloody Thatcher woman ever was, and He shall walk upon the floors of the Stock Exchange and eject all He finds there, crying, "You're just a bunch of overprivileged little parasites who do worship mammon above the Lord your God and do designer drugs! Hie thee hence to repent your loathsome ways, you public school bastards! For surely, it is harder for a chinless little spiv in a Paul Smith suit to enter the Kingdom of Heaven, than for a camel to pass through the eye of a needle!"

'And as the final days approach, and all is majesty upon the Earth (except for parts of Liverpool, which are beyond even God's powers to glorify), the dead shall rise and there will be many who will go, "Eurrgh! What's that awful smell?" and the dead will be truly embarrassed.

'And God shall say unto man, "Rejoice!"... and man shall say unto God, "That's easy for you to say! You're not down here with them! They smell disgusting and jump out when we least expect it and go 'Boo!', which they think is extraordinarily funny for some reason, and you can hardly move in Sainsbury's on Saturdays for throngs of the dead buying deodorants and giant economy bottles of embalming fluids!"

'And God shall remain silent on this one, and leave the living to just get on with it.

'And then, upon the day of 31 August 1999, Gabriel shall sound His horn and people shall cry out, "Hey! Knock it off! There are people trying to sleep!" But all shall rise to see God in all His glory in the firmament. And people shall say, "Bloody Hell! He really is an old man with a long white beard after all! If I was God, I think I'd make myself look like Tom Cruise rather than Catweazle!"

'And God shall be annoyed at this criticism of His majestic person, and all the television stations will go off the air simultaneously, in the middle of a good programme.

'And upon the roof of the world shall appear the Twelve Horsemen of the Apocalypse – yea, twelve, because St John of Revelation couldst not count for shit. And their names shall be Death, Famine, Pestilence, Plague, War, Dicky Tummy, Impotence, Waiting for a Bus at

Night, Snooker, Passive Smoking, Pretty Girls Who Won't Go Out with You, Jimmy, Frederick and Tony.

'And the world shall be rent asunder by their passing. And God shall say, "How's that for an Apocalypse, mortals! Now it is time for the Day of Judgement to commence!

'"Come forth ye worshippers of mammon, ye pervie-coveters of neighbours' oxen and purveyors of MFI furniture, ye followers of Satan or Manchester United, ye readers of smutty books in the toilets and potting sheds of the world, ye writers of dubious comedy books for Christmas and ye readers thereof and all ye responsible for administering the poll tax.

'"And come estate agents and solicitors, and ye train spotters who didst piss down the drain the precious time which your Lord gave you on Earth. Assemble the false prophets who said Alfie Brookes doesn't know his arse from his elbow, because it doth transpire that he does!

'"And come ye who are called Cheryl, Kevin, Wayne, Sharon, Tracy and Clint, for your names are an abomination in the eyes of the Lord! Oh, and everyone called Kylie as well.

'"Come ye... um... Who else?" And the Lord shall pause a moment and cup His chin in a mighty palm a hundred miles across. "Well, come the lot of ye, for thou art doubtlessly all sinners."

'And Jesus will interject upon Mankind's behalf, saying, "Dad, go easy on them, for they know not what they've done, especially those accused of pervie-coveting their neighbour's oxen. Be a bit more New Testament and start dishing out the forgiveness."

'And God shall reply unto Jesus: "I doth not want this lot with Us in the Kingdom of Heaven, especially pervie-coveters of oxen and train spotters! Most assuredly can Satan have the lot of them! I don't give a stuff!"

'Jesus shall cry unto Heaven and God shall answer, "Look, who's God around here, You or Me?" And Jesus shall answer, "That's a complex theological issue, but if I do understand it right, We both are. And I say save all those who will come unto Me!"

'And God will protest, but eventually He shall say unto the assembled multitude: "Right, all those who want to be saved, go unto Jesus, because He's more forgiving than I ever would be!"

'And all shall run unto Jesus and be saved – except for the lame and the crippled and the old and sick, who canst not make it in time and so are eternally damned... but then, life's a bitch like that, isn't it?'

Alfie has started coming out of his rapture and is shambling over to his gas cooker to put the kettle on.

We have a cup of tea with him, our heads reeling with his vivid images of the Apocalypse, while he dunks rich tea biscuits and digs absent-mindedly at his earwax with a probing finger.

'I hope you boys got what you came for,' he says to us at the door. 'It's nice to have visitors. I don't know anyone around here, so drop by if you're ever in these parts again!'

We tell him we will, shake hands and make to leave.

As we step outside into the brisk afternoon air, we pause to wonder for a moment, looking Heavenwards, up into eternity, and pondering all we've heard. But then it starts to rain, so we go home.

PREDICTIONS EVEN WE DON'T BELIEVE...

While researching this book we heard thousands of staggering predictions for the 1990s, many of which we felt were just too far-fetched to ever come true. But who knows?

● Two members of Bros will join Mensa.

● Prince Charles will divorce Princess Diana and move in with Danny DeVito.

● People in England and Wales will greatly benefit from the introduction of the poll tax.

● The Labour Party will win the next General Election.

● After frantic talks with his PR advisors, Michael Jackson will agree to withdraw his newly released cover version of *I'm Forever Blowing Bubbles.*

● Bradford will be torn apart in 1993 by bloody 'Pork Scratching' riots, as Moslem Fundamentalists, grossly insulted by this snack made from 'An unclean beast of the trotter', demand it to be banned as an affront to their beliefs.

● In 1994 they will riot again, burning TV sets after Channel 4 re-runs *Pinky and Perky* and a particularly provocative Danish bacon commercial.

● In 1995 they will riot again, furious at the wanton display of womens' hair in a Head & Shoulders commercial.

● Terry Waite (and all the other hostages) will be released.

● In 1996 the Moslem Fundamentalists will riot again in protest against Channel 4's *Right to Reply,* incensed by free speech which is an affront to their beliefs.

● Iran will not start World War 3.

● The alphabet will be rearranged and 'G' will become the 20th letter.

● President Bush will do something (this is predicted for 1993).